Nancy Schreimann

THE SCIENCE
OF FINDING A JOB

A Step by Step Guide to Job Hunting Success

The Science of Finding a Job: A Step By Step Guide to Job Hunting Success

Written by Nancy Schreimann

The Science of Finding a Job

First Edition

Copyright © **2012** Nancy Schreimann

All rights reserved.

ISBN **978-0-615-72621-2**

Copyright and Registered Trademarks and References in this book

This book contains references to several web based businesses and some products. For purposes of clarification, the names/products listed below are registered trademarks in the United States and possibly other countries. Included in this list are:

Microsoft Word®
Microsoft Excel®
Linkedin®
FaceBook® is a registered trademark of FaceBook, Inc.
Hoover's™
Experian ®
TransUnion ®
Equifax®
Onesource ™
Google ™

Table of Contents –

Foreword: Job Seeking As a Science

A lot of people think searching for a job has more elements of luck, timing and personality than it does planning. You just "happen" to get an interview with a good company versus a mediocre company, or you just "happen" to discover a job opening the day you are looking, or someone looks at your resume and, as luck would have it, likes what they see. You get the job offer and you might even believe it's due to your personality or having all the "right" answers, but you never really "know" why or how you got the job versus someone else. After all, you don't know who else interviewed or any of the things they said or did. There are a million reasons why you might have won or lost the job, and as you move forward with your career you might look back and hope you can guess what you did right so you can keep doing the same thing the next time and have the same luck.

Well, the truth is, luck and timing DO play a part in finding a job and keeping one. But what you do and how you do it has a lot to do with whether or not you realize success in your job search. Opportunity is where planning and hard work meet up with luck and timing. People who are successful seem to find success again and again, and it's often because they place themselves in a position where the timing and opportunity are right. They do that through planning and action. Planning and action are the secret sauce to finding a job, getting the interview and saying the right things, negotiating the right salary and fitting in to that company once you get there. Having and maintaining a network of acquaintances, friends, and business contacts is a critical ingredient to making sure you get that opportunity at the right time. So it all boils down to planning, and that is how this book will help. Having a documented plan when it's time for the job search is key and after reading this book you will be able to develop a set of actionable plans to follow that will lead to that job success.

It's also important to stay motivated during a job search. Many people complain that they send out resumes over and over and get no response. No one will return their emails or calls. After applying to every possible posted position, they give up. After all, they have tried everything, right? Actually, this approach to applying for job is primarily a waste of time, so most people have little success. Rather, the best approach involves a combination of personal and business contacts, knowledge of who is hiring and for what positions, and creative presentation of you for the company/position. One way to stay motivated is to have a solid plan, then have a backup plan and a backup plan for that. This is something I refer to as *Plan ABCDE*. At least five plans allows you to cycle through a plan, then if this plan doesn't bear fruit, moving to a second plan, and so on. This is an important approach to staying motivated; you will be plenty busy working through your plans and won't have time to give up.

I read in the newspaper almost every day about the difficulty of finding a job and how people suddenly find themselves out of work and are one paycheck away from losing their home. People can and do fall on hard times, but can all these people really be victims of bad luck and a down economy? I don't believe there are many times when a job loss should be a surprise. People should know if management thinks they are not doing a good job, if customers aren't buying the product their company sells, if their industry is having financial difficulties, if the company has poor financial results or if there are layoffs planned. Companies have different cultures; some have a layoff culture and some do not. If yours has a layoff culture, know that you are at risk. The main factor to keeping your job is placing yourself in a position whenever possible where you are not going to be eliminated. And when you know the gig is up, you should be preparing and planning in advance for the new job search. Keep your network current at all times, regardless of how well you feel you are doing at your existing job. You never know when a better opportunity could present itself or when your current employer and job could change to a more negative situation.

Why is looking for a job a science and not an art? An art is creating a plan as you go along. Art is a creative act where you discover and improvise. A science is a series of steps that produce the same result each time. Would you rather have your job search be an art or a science? Most people are looking desperately for the steps they should follow so that they can achieve the end result of obtaining a decent job and keeping that job. A science has a meticulous list of tasks, in the right sequential order or concurrently if that is what is required. It's the same process every time you do it; there is a right way to be sure your outcome will be a success. If you follow this scientific approach, you will have higher odds of success finding a job. You will put yourself in a position to be successful. You will be able to better keep your motivation up with a checklist of action items.

The reality is that there have been books and articles that talk about business leaders, professional athletes, or famous people and how they got where they are. The saying is that there are 10,000 hours of practice and intense focus and many failures before these people saw success. These people believed in their ability to be successful and deter negative input by firmly focusing on their goals. In short, they had a plan and intended to be successful. You should do the same in your job search: a positive attitude and belief in yourself are critical.

In order to create these plans with the related action items, and prioritize the plans, you will need to follow the process step by step and keep a documented action plan.

It's best to do this on a computer as you might modify these plans or move them around when priorities change. Eventually the process will become second nature to you. You will become confident and self-assured about your ability to find a position that fits your skills and goals and, better; keep that position until you want to conduct a new search for a different job.

Section 1: Foundation Planning ABCDE

By the end of Foundation, you should have a solid Plan A, B, C, D and E (Five plans) for your job search. You will have identified:

- What jobs you are suited for and what jobs interest you
- Identifying the places you might want to work and live
- Identified which Companies have jobs that fit your job search list (i.e. type of job, locations)
- Identified what people you know who can help you in your job search
- Researched companies and opportunities in your locations of choice
- Prepared multiple resumes for specific types of jobs
- Ordered the priority of your search A, B, C, D, and E (five plans).

Planning to find a job is the most important part of the process for finding a job. Planning involves covering a lot of different areas before you do anything. The reason for this is to ensure that you don't run out of steam or motivation before you have achieved success. Have you ever been to a large dinner buffet? We often start at one end and start filling our plate. When the plate is full, we sit down and eat. We then go back to where we left off and find out that many of the items further down the buffet were foods we would rather have eaten, but we are too full. So the point is, survey the buffet BEFORE you start eating, make sure you know where you want to spend your time first, second and so forth. This is the concept behind planning and prioritizing your time. Additionally, when doing a thorough plan, you will find there are a lot of options and you can focus on the important ones first, so you don't miss opportunities by focusing on the wrong things. Some people believe you just take action, but taking action with no plan often ends with failure and with no planning, failure can be depleting and deflating; you may lose your motivation to proceed.

Planning Step 1: Creating a List of Job Positions

The purpose of this section is to identify a list of jobs that would fit your skills and interests.
You may not be aware of all the types of jobs available to someone with your skills. So it's important to figure out what types of jobs you *should* pursue. There is no point in applying for jobs where you have no skills match.

You can start by **Brainstorming** or listing position types and then under each type, several subtypes where you might be a fit. Ask yourself the following questions...
Did I take a training course or obtain a college degree in a specific field? If so, what is the list of jobs where my degree or certification might apply?
Example: Suppose you have a general Marketing degree. The types of jobs you might perform include

- Sales: What types of sales would you be qualified for due to interest or experience? Retail, technology sales, pharmaceutical sales, car sales etc.? Do you have knowledge of any of these product areas?
- Consulting: Is there an area of experience such as retail, supply chain, or technology where you might be a subject matter expert or have extensive interest? For example, if you have an accounting or finance degree, could you learn about some of the financial computer systems from major vendors, then apply that as a functional (Subject matter not technology) expert in that area.
- Marketing: This type of job includes working in a marketing department, website marketing, social media marketing, potentially advertising etc.
- Business: This general type of job could include working in different departments such as Human Resources, Engineering, Marketing, Support, Maintenance, Shop Floor, Information Technology, Accounting and Finance, Procurement, Supply Chain or Logistics (transportation and distribution).

Write down every job title and type of job you can think of where you might be qualified due to your education, degree, or experience (if you did an internship or worked for a prior company). If you don't know, your college career office at the University you attended is an option. Doing a search on the internet under "marketing jobs" for example, may surface many types of positions.

What type of jobs did you work at in High School or College summers?
- Did you work for a family member?
- Did you volunteer?
- Did you get CPR certification?
- Did you raise money for an organization?

- Did you babysit or work in preschool?
- Give swimming lessons? Coach sports?
- Wait tables?
- Did you work on the yearbook?
- Work in construction, paint houses?
- Mow lawns?
- Start your own home based business?

For all of these types of jobs, what experience did you get that might apply to a career? Would you be willing to consider a similar job to one you had in the past? From this question, you should retain a list of job skills that can translate to a set of skills that can be utilized in other positions, as well as possibly generate a list of jobs you might be willing to do again, even if shorter term. Think of the skills you might use in a career, such as responsibilities around opening or closing activities, supervising others, training new employees, etc.

You will now start creating a list of Skills and Achievements. The purpose of this effort is to associate a list of potential jobs that could potentially leverage these skills.

This one may seem difficult, because many times the jobs we hold in High School or afterwards don't seem to apply to our field of study in college. Perhaps not, but the *skills* learned, might be applied. Skills such as management, organization, leadership, rewards/recognition for job done above and beyond the requirements. Perhaps some examples might help.

- While in college, Bob and Steve started a business buying older cars, fixing them up and selling them on the internet. Bob and Steve made $20,000 per year selling these cars, money they split and saved, using some to reinvest in more cars. The skills obtained by Bob and Steve were purchasing, marketing, finance, collections, and sales. They learned how to run their own business. They had to research what to buy, what to pay, what price to sell the product for and then find a buyer. They had to reinvest their gains wisely.
    - o Jobs that might be good for Bob and Steve where these skills would be valued could be a purchasing agent, working for a car dealership or large multi-dealership agency, working in finance or financial analysis, or working in a sales role.
- Ally babysat since she was 12. When she turned 17, she was hired to work summer camp programs at a school. Ally was the lead teacher for the kids in her assigned classes. Skills she learned were developing a schedule, lesson

plans/daily plans, creating and managing a schedule, leading a team, and course development. She was a trustworthy and dependable person with the children, keeping the kids engaged and safe. She was a trusted leader to the school management since they allowed her to lead the effort.

- o Jobs that might be good for Ally would be a YMCA or Camp teacher, working a child program lead for a church, working at a school as a counselor, teaching, and working in a training organization in a company.

After brainstorming within your own mind, you might brainstorm with people you know who work in fields that interest you. Ask the people you know what type of jobs they have in their company for people with your background and your degree. They may bring up ideas you never thought about.

Possibly you feel you don't know anyone, meaning, you don't think you know someone who has the type of professional job you would consider. However, you DO know more people than you think you know. Section 2, Contact List will elaborate on this concept much further, helping you to reach deep into your family, friends, church, school, work and other groups to create a network of contacts. For the purposes of this section, you need to start figuring out what types of jobs are out there and to do that, you have to talk to people.

Ask yourself, who are my closest friends, people I just know (fraternity brothers, people you played football with in High School, neighbors, and people at your church, people you work with at temporary jobs). What do those people do for a living now? What type of work are their parents doing? Their siblings and other family members? (If you don't know, ask them). Do the parents have any friends or acquaintances who work in the field of X (your preferred field) or at a Company that is well known and respected? If so, would they mind brokering an introduction for you so you can explore the type of jobs in that field? (That is your only goal right now, you are not reaching out to these people to try and get a job interview, and you simply want "their advice" or "their opinion" about areas in their company or field of work that might offer an opportunity later for someone like yourself).

This may seem a far reaching effort and maybe seems pointless at this time; however, it's far from pointless. It helps you begin a list of contacts, acquaintances, friends and others who could help you later when the search is on full force. You can learn a lot by talking to someone who works at a company about the types of jobs and opportunities at that company. Below is a solid example from my own experience.

I received a call from a family friend who had stayed in close touch with many friends over thirty years, many of whom resided in the Chicago area. One of the friends's had a son who was graduating college within a year and he was trying to understand what type of finance jobs might be available at large companies in the technology industry. The son learned that I and my husband both worked for large technology companies and had been in the industry for 28 years. He forwarded his resume to my relative asking if he could talk to me about jobs he saw posted on the web from my current employer. I said sure, I'd help him out.

What proceeded from there was a scheduled conversation with this young man, who had an accounting degree. He had applied for some jobs for pre-sales engineers that were local to his hometown. I told him this position was far reaching, and in my opinion he wouldn't even get to an interview because he didn't match the qualifications. I told him there were other jobs that were posted on the internal job postings at the company. (Most large companies must first post any jobs internally before they look outside the firm. Often these jobs are filled not by miscellaneous external candidates but by *people they know who work there and have directly referred them.*)

I asked the young man if he would be willing to move and what places he would be willing to work. He hadn't thought about this (note that is something we are going to know when you have this conversation). I looked online and identified a fair number of entry-level jobs for people of his background. All required 5+ years of experience. As he had done three internships, I felt this qualified as some experience if not 5 years. *I cut and pasted the job descriptions into an email.* I pointed out what they were looking for regarding skills.

Next I reviewed his resume, which was a typical college resume; list of education, with work experience following, then hobbies. I mentioned to the young man that in my opinion his resume would fail to obtain him an interview as it had *no career goal that matched the job description. Education was listed first which indicates no work experience,* and the *wording didn't match the type of skills the job description requested.* I sent him my resume as a sample and indicated a rewrite was in order. He was somewhat put off, because he just wanted to find a job, <u>and had been sure that he would not have to do anything other than make the contact and turn in the canned resume.</u> He did not think about making a real plan, or having a step-by-step job hunting procedure.

I thought to myself "this poor fellow has no clue how to get a job. He doesn't recognize that it was rare to have anyone take the time to provide this quality of mentoring." However, he responded that he would work on it and scheduled a follow up call with me the next week. In the meantime, I noted the internal job ads had no hiring manager name on them (they often have both the internal recruiter and the hiring manager name). The recruiter would screen out candidates but the hiring manager will take a referral and tell the recruiter to talk to the person.

A few days later, I was at a local event in my town with an old friend from the technology industry. We ran into a lady there who he introduced as someone from the finance department at the technology company. I had never met her before. This person had been promoted to a national level job in the finance area. I asked her briefly about the type of positions I'd noticed in our internal job listing. These positions *reported to her.* I asked if she would consider reviewing a recent graduate. She said if I felt it was worth her time, she would have the recruiter call this young man, i.e. *with my recommendation she would give him a shot.* I then proceeded to send her his resume the following week, and it was the old resume, not an edited one. I did this because he did not call me on the scheduled date, nor provide me the updated resume. She replied that the recruiter would give him a call.

What followed this activity is the most interesting part of the story. I emailed the young man and indicated the recruiter was going to call him about the position. At this point, there are so many things that could have happened to the benefit of this young man. What he should have done and what he didn't do are two different discussions. What he didn't do was;

- Respond back thanking me for my help and promising to follow up with the outcome (Note, I get paid a referral fee for people who I get hired, so there was something in it for me financially). Also, I wanted to make this recent graduate a personal contact and add it to my business contacts, after all, I had two kids in college who may need the same favor someday.
- Respond back to me with the updated resume in a timely manner, the one that had a career goal and skills description that fit the job in the ad. I did inform him to do this, sent him my resume as a sample, but a week went by with no response.
- Didn't follow up with me after any calls he got, so I have no idea if he had an interview, if it went well or didn't go well, why or why not.
- Didn't follow up with me at all. Primarily, before *the interview over the phone* to get advice about what to say and not to say, what type of areas to emphasize and some reasons and research about why he might be interested in working for THIS Company? Nor did he follow-up after the interview.
- Probably (guessing based on inaction) that he didn't do *the appropriate research* on the company, i.e. what the company sells, how the company makes money, is the company driven by sales, operations, or by customer service (culture type of consideration) and how HE might fit into the culture of this company.

- Probably (guess based on the inaction) that he didn't write a thank you note to the recruiter after the conversation, and didn't get to the interview stage because I never heard anything back from this contact at the company about him.

Note: successful people **do things that other people don't feel like doing.** This doesn't imply these less successful people are just lazy folks, they aren't always, but they skip steps, don't feel like doing what it takes, or worse, don't really know what to do and don't ask anyone. The purpose of this book is to inform people about what they ought to do to be successful. This young man clearly didn't know what to do or worse, just didn't feel like doing it.

As a result of this experience, I also learned something. I learned that I shouldn't stick my neck out for just anyone. I should wait and see if they show follow-up and a genuine interest. I'm not sure how the conversation went with this young man or if it ever took place, but I would be embarrassed should I run into this new financial contact at my company and find out that this college graduate didn't follow up with her either, or didn't appear interested. That just makes me look bad. She wouldn't probably take another referral from me, so now someone else who genuinely deserved an opportunity might not get the opportunity.

All of the things you SHOULD do are listed in this book, and if you choose not to do them, then that is your decision. But realize, when you decide not to do the right thing, you are hurting your ability to get a job in the future. Because I can assure you, I would never help this young man again, at my company or refer him to other people I know in this industry, and after 28 years, I know a LOT of people.

Finally, to complete your list of jobs and descriptions, you need to do some research. This research can easily be done over the Internet. You can visit job boards, company sites where you know there are jobs in the areas of interest, or go to specialty job sites (financial jobs, sales jobs, etc, there are numerous sites that specialize in jobs for one field of business) and read through the job postings. Note the *title* for these jobs and note the *job descriptions, verbiage used in the descriptions.* You might print some of these out and keep the job descriptions for use in later sections on preparing the resume for the job application process. Add the titles to your list of jobs that might suit you. Make note/link the websites that seem to offer positions of interest.

The outcome of this step then will be a list of your skills and accomplishments and a long list of potential jobs where you might have a fit, including the common titles for these jobs.

Planning Step 2: Identifying the Places You Might Want to Work and Live

Now that you have created a list of potential jobs that suit your skills and interests, it's important to identify companies who might have these jobs available, including small local firms as well as large multi-national firms. The best approach to identifying the companies is to first identify where you might be willing to live.

If you have not thought about this, it's highly important. Many people think they will search around the area where they grew up or where their current home is located. Doing this can be part of the bigger plan, however, it's very restricting, since in many locations the job opportunities can be few and the job opportunities *in your field* can be significantly limited. If you have opened your mind to other options, you might consider other locations where you can live, even commute, if local positions are all that you have considered. The following are the criteria for consideration of a place to live and work (your order, your priority):

- Family/Friends located nearby.
- Housing (affordable homes or rental options).
- Cost of Living (some larger cities the cost can be 2-3x the cost of a smaller city)
- Climate/Weather.
- Like the city (been there, visited or lived there at one time in the past).
- Size of city/town.
- Would be willing to live in this place a few years only.
- Distance from home town.
- A lot of job opportunities in this place due to size of city, or the location of many firms in this city.
- Spouse or significant other willing to live there.
- Schools are good and close by the location if applicable.
- Desperation; i.e. you need a job and would be willing to go anywhere to get one.

In general, most people pick a place they prefer to live (often close to hometown or family) and start applying there, then, as the job search is unsuccessful, cast a wider net of places to search. This approach can be discouraging because the further away the job search from any familiar place, the less motivating or successful the job search. As the search moves away from the preferred job location, the other locations receive short shrift and are more likely to be on-line or non-specific searches. Many companies are hesitant to hire someone who lives far from the job location, because the person needs to relocate, meaning there may be baggage (family, house, or other issues) and the person may end up unhappy in the new location, may not know people or be a good fit for that location. That is why companies often interview local people for local jobs, but when faced with few options, *move a person from within the company to that location before they hire someone from outside the firm to move to the location.*

The reason for applying for a job position in any location should never be desperation. It should always be thought out, focused and selected location for the search. People will ask you during the interview why their company, that location, that position. You need to have a pointed and honest answer, and if you do this research now, you can clearly state that you reviewed the opportunities and the cities where you wanted to live and identified *this company, this position and this city* as a fit.

For this section, you need to go back to some of your former job boards or web sites for specific job types. Where were the jobs located? Are any of these cities places where you might want to live? In general, the best places to live are larger cities/states because there are more companies headquartered or clustered in major cities. But the opposite could also apply; small towns need certain types of skills for their businesses, and these skills might be scarce. Some cities to consider where there might be a lot of jobs include; Atlanta, Georgia; Chicago, Illinois; Washington DC, Virginia/Maryland surrounding corridor; New York and New Jersey area (an hour from major city locations at most); Denver, Colorado; Dallas, Texas; and San Francisco, California and others. Secondary cities where there would be plentiful jobs might include Redmond, Washington; Miami, Florida; Birmingham, Alabama; St. Louis, Missouri; Minneapolis, Minnesota; Boston, Massachusetts; Philadelphia, Pennsylvania; Los Angeles, California, and others. What you will find is that in some locations, there are more jobs than in others. It's important to note that living in some of these places means you can change jobs in your field more easily and go to other companies with the experience you have gained. A smaller town might not have the opportunity to allow you to move around within your field and if you are suddenly out of work, you might get "stuck" in that location.

Have a good and focused answer prepared as to why that city or town is on your top choice list. Saying you are interested in that company or industry, or stating you lived there before or had friends there would be sufficient.

Once you make a list of the locations where the jobs on your list seem plentiful, or where there are a lot of companies that seem to be advertising in that location, make the list as complete as possible. You might prioritize this list based on your findings from the job postings on your job types from section 1, along with what you know or prefer about the locations. Researching the companies hiring and the jobs available in these cities is the next chapter, so it's important to narrow down a list that includes about 10-20 places you would be willing to live at minimum. Prioritize these locations into highest to lowest preferences. Having only one or two is far too limiting and having 50-100 is far too many for research purposes.

If you need help, it might be important to reach out to people you know who have lived in these cities or still live there. Ask them about the quality of life. Cost of living, transportation, schools and job opportunities in these places. Find out what companies are big in these cities. Knowing someone there can be a big help when trying to navigate a new marketplace. Also, it could help with identifying contacts that they know who might help you in your job search in that location.

Planning Step 3: What Companies Have Jobs That Fit Your Job Search List?

You have already started this list, because primarily, you have gone out to job boards, company web sites, and pulled job descriptions that helped you create a list of potential job positions and descriptions. You might have noticed the company names that have these job listings posted. Most job postings have also a location or list of locations where they want to fill these positions.

Starting with your highest priority locations, you will need to do a fair amount of research to discover what companies are headquartered in the city /state where you want to live; what companies are "hiring" for this location; and where you can find out about the jobs or expansions that might be taking place in these locations. To do this you might have to spend some time and some money getting online subscriptions to the following sources

- **Newspapers (Main newspaper for the cities where you are interested in living).** There may be job listings in the classifieds of a newspaper but these postings are not necessarily representative of the opportunities in these areas. Reading the business section of the newspaper tells you more about the companies there, including articles about expansion and companies moving to the area. One example of information in a newspaper (local) has a list of public companies and their stock tickers in that city. You can create a list of companies and then do some research on them, look at their job postings and see if there is any type of fit with the jobs of interest.

- **Business Magazines (Many cities or states have a business magazine that highlights business activity around the state).** Two examples of these might be *Florida Trend*, and *Atlanta Business Journal.* You can go to *Bizjournals.com* and subscribe to multiple online journals. These journals are highly useful because they typically list activity by county in the business arena, such as who is expanding, who is hiring, and articles by CEOs and other leaders. This information can be very useful in finding out what companies are there, who is hiring and what they are looking to do regarding expansion. These Journals have both larger and smaller companies covered in their articles. Considering a small company could mean a chance to try multiple jobs roles and possibly take on more responsibility.

- **Hoovers or One Source.** Hoovers or OneSource are two electronic sources for all kinds of useful information. These are fee based subscription that may allow a free period. You may only need to subscribe to these services for the duration of your job search or if you are really short on cash, only for the first few months of research. Once you have a company list, you will need to research the companies more deeply. Hoovers has the names of key executives and key employees, including often their email and phone numbers. The site also covers what these companies do, who their competitors are, and their financial condition. The financial condition is important, because a company who is in financial trouble may not be able to offer any longer term job security for you. You should stick with companies who have growth potential and are in stable financial condition. (I.e. revenues are increasing annually and balance sheet shows cash on hand, profit exceeding losses longer term).

- **Web Sites.** Once you know that a company of interest resides in your city or state of prioritization, you should just go to their website and take a look at what they do, what jobs are posted, and any recent news. Usually press releases, news, financial reports and even links to a financial presentation video or material are available in the "about the company" section of a web site. Recent news is key as often these articles provide names of key executives and provide a reference for conversation when interviewing at the company. People like to know that you have some information about the company and your application wasn't just random. You could print or copy and store on your computer or create a link to a few of these articles because you might need them later when coming up with contacts or before the interview.

- **Job Board by location (job boards general and specific to your field):** Other web sites to explore might include job boards that are specific to your title or type of job/industry. There are job boards for financial positions, sales positions, positions in the oil and gas industry etc. You can search them on *Google* or any search engine. These boards ought to be a great reference for you to explore the companies hiring in your cities of choice and to identify recruiters who specialize in these industries. There are also job boards that are for a specific location, such as XYZ (city name) jobs. Search for these as well. The local job boards may contain lower level or temporary positions, or you might notice a lot of the listings are for temp firms. But a temp firm can be an option for getting in the door. So note these companies (temp firms) as well as companies headquartered or hiring in your city/state of choice.

After you have a list of companies, job listings /descriptions and associated companies from the job boards, you should start to create a file of job descriptions by type along with company names who offer these jobs in your locations of interest.

You should organize these either by location or by job type. This really depends on if location is flexible but you prefer specific job types.

An example, if you have a financial or accounting degree you might have audit/tax type job descriptions, financial analytics or system analyst type of jobs, consulting for financials, or controller/accounting descriptions. You will need these job descriptions later, but you should put them into categories and keep at least 5-10 job descriptions per job type. Make note of the companies listed who are hiring these job types. It may be recruiters (independent) or you may have found the positions on a web site of a company.

At this point, you should have:

- A list of job titles and job descriptions
- A list of locations where you want to work in priority order
- An associated list of companies located in these locations, including those who happened to have a job posted in your field of interest.
- A grouping of job title priorities to sort these in, or location priorities for organization.
  - Example. Location would be first choice location, second choice location, third choice location and all associated companies and job descriptions you found under each location
  - Example. Job Title or Main field of Interest. List of types of positions (Sales, Financial Analysis, Consulting, Corporate finance) with job descriptions/companies under these that are selected from *the locations where you are willing to live.*

Planning Step 4: Who You Know Who Can Help You in Your Job Search

Your contact list is a critical step in the job search process. Everyone has a contact list of people they know: acquaintances, business associates, old friends, parents of friends and so on. These people either work in, have worked in, or at least know someone who works in a company where you might find a job. Most companies hire first from referrals and second from other sources such as colleges, recruiters and direct applicants. The key is to find out *how* to get referred and obtain as many referrals as possible. Of course it helps if you are focused on a list of locations, and a list of companies in those locations. Now your goal is to track down people who work in these locations and/or work in the companies you have identified in these locations.

Many people use **social networks** heavily today to create a list of contacts and to search for jobs. It's actually quite effective and will be covered more extensively later in this book. The two most widely used are *FaceBook* for family and friends and for professionals *LinkedIn*. My recommendation LATER in this book is to create a LinkedIn profile, but this should be done once you complete the next chapter, *Have Resumes Prepared for the Job Titles*. Once you have several resumes prepared, you might take your best career objective, job type listings and skills and use that to build out a creative on-line resume. You will then proceed to link to many of your contacts, and additionally, to many of the professionals at company names you have identified should they have a LinkedIn page. You can do the same on FaceBook (friend the company) but before you do, you will need to clean up your own FaceBook page extensively. (This will be covered later.) Do a search on your name and see what pops up. Likely you either show up at the bottom of the search or you show up as the FaceBook or LinkedIn profile you have on line. Make sure there are no negative references to your name.

For purposes of this step, *who you Know for the job search*, try to use the contacts you already have on FaceBook to obtain the information on the below questions. You can reach out to these friends individually (no blast to the group) and ask for the information. Remember that you have an online "reputation" which comes from the groups you are associated with and the people /pictures you are friended/linked with. If the reputation is casual (non-professional) that is ok, as long as it's not negative or associated with people who spend all day posting everything they do on line including hourly activities, or "hanging out" online commenting on every possible thing. People who send a lot of twitter messages or keep a constant blog entry might be viewed as too tied to social media to focus on a job. So stop the constant chatter and do not link to anyone who has any negative reputation, pictures, or anything else that could reflect on you negatively. This type of behavior of being online and constantly sending or updating messages is highly unprofessional and may dissuade a hiring manager from even considering you for a job. It makes you appear to be someone who doesn't have a life offline. So please start thinking about that NOW, and start cleaning up your online presence so that there are no links into people or groups that might cause recruiters to consider you trivial or non-focused on professional activities during daytime hours.

The contact list is also an important source in Section 2 that follows, "Using the contact list to get *Your Name Out There.*" The contact list is people you know, friends of friends, acquaintances, parents of friends, people who attend your church/Gym/Clubs, neighbors, prior employment friends, bosses, teachers, fraternity brothers and so on.

You need to now start to develop a contact list. Start with a list of people from the above sources, call or email people, tell them you are looking for a job in X industry in Y city or at Z Company, and since they work in that company, city or industry, could they advise you on the following:

- What kind of jobs are available at their company? In their industry?
- What jobs should I be applying for? If they have some suggestions on what jobs, then you can ask, "Do you know who is responsible for hiring for these types of jobs?"
- What are the open job requisitions posted?
- Who is the hiring manager for the job posted?
- Where are they hiring (location)?
- How long has the job been open? (The more recent, the better).
- What is the job description i.e. what are the requirements for this position? Can you email me the job description so I understand what skills they are looking for?
- Does the contact know anyone who currently has this job or is hiring for these types of jobs (even if it's not the same person who has the open opportunity), if so, they can ask their contact what type of candidates are of interest/ does that person know the hiring manager and what do they know about the manager? (They may offer to reach out to the hiring manager on your behalf or not, put off asking for now).

- Most importantly, would they be willing in the future to submit your resume to the job openings posted or send it to someone internally on your behalf?

It may seem out of line to ask some people these questions however, understand that in many larger companies *a referral bonus is paid* when the company hires someone they refer. This bonus is usually $1000-$3500. So the person will or should be motivated to refer someone who seems qualified. Also, when the conversation is around you wanting "their advice" or "their opinion" few people will fail to offer their advice or opinion. If you are on the other hand, asking for a "favor" from someone you don't really know, they will likely look for a way to get out of the conversation. That is why you need to practice what you will say and how you will say it. Role play with friends or parents. Some sample conversations might be:

- Ask the minister at your church if he knows who in the congregation works in the area of (as an example) finance or accounting because you are looking for some advice on the best opportunities in this field. The minister might then walk you over and introduce you to Susan Jones and Steve Simpson. Susan is a CFO at a small local firm, and Steve is an Auditor for a large accounting firm. You might then ask when it would be a good time to either sit down in person for 30 minutes (no more) or on the phone to ask them about the jobs in their industry as you are creating a list of potential opportunities and could use some advice. You are likely to get that meeting, because the minister provided the introduction and you didn't tell them you were looking for a job. If you said that you were looking for a job, most responses would be "I'm not the hiring manager" or "send me your resume and Ill forward it on" or "call John Jones in our hiring department". Again, you don't want this type of help right now because these type of responses are known as "blow-offs". When someone doesn't offer to *personally handle your introduction* then they are not going to help you other than to give you a name.

- Ask your friends or acquaintances what type of work their parents do and what companies they work for. If for example, Fred's dad works as a foreman in construction for a small family firm, you might still ask him if you can have a minute to obtain his advice on "finance type jobs" in the industry where he works. For all you know, Fred's Dad used to work for a larger firm and happens to know the Controller there. This type of info is invaluable for your use later. Remember, you are gathering contacts, NOT applying for jobs or asking for favors. So just note this info but nothing else for now.

- Sometimes, you might find that someone's father, mother or friend knows someone who works at a company on your list. In that case, you might find out if that person is willing to advise you about opportunities at that company. You can even show them the position list and tell them the types of positions you are exploring. If the opportunity presents itself, you can ask this person for a personal introduction. Meaning, they can send an email to their friend and tell that person you are interested in their company, and wanted some "advice" on how best to apply there. Again, you need to put it into these terms, you are not asking this person to provide you inside help, and you are simply looking for advice. During these discussions, asking the questions above, you will find out if the company is hiring, where (location) and how best to apply. The person might offer to help you and if they do, ask them to help you understand the job descriptions and contact information for the positions. Nothing else for now, you are not ready to interview because when you are ready, you can't afford to make ANY mistakes. You must have the right resume, the right research on the company and what specific skills the company/hiring manager is looking for, and the right (if possible) contacts/sponsorship.

- If you have any contacts who found a job in your field, perhaps people you know who graduated in your class or were acquaintances from college, you might reach out to them directly if you still have their information. Mention an interest in the company where they work and wanting some advice about what made their job search successful. Find out how they got the job and what they did right and what advice they would give you to up your chances.

This process may take a few weeks of calling and talking to people. This requires a personal approach, (try not to text at all, email might be ok,) but phone or face to face is better. It's not haphazard, it's planned, and you try to cover all the bases so that you create a long list of contact names, who can help you later when you are ready to apply for jobs.

Planning Step 5: Research and Find Opportunities Posted At the Companies in Your Locations of Choice

In earlier chapters, you should have gathered a fair amount of information that can be used to help you with this portion of your planning. You know the locations you prefer and you have come up with an initial list of titles and job descriptions. You have spoken to and identified some contacts already who may be working at some of these companies or who may know someone there. You have subscribed to publications and have *started documenting a list of companies that are headquartered or have significant offices in your cities/states of choice,* including any that were advertising or expanding and might be hiring (read about it in the business journal or newspaper or saw the job postings on their website or elsewhere). Having a comprehensive list of potential employers is key, because this will help greatly in directing your search to companies who offer positions in your areas of expertise.

It's up to you on how this information is managed: you can print it out or keep an electronic file. The information should be organized in some way, such as by location or by job title. I personally prefer to print out a one page description of the companies, then print out the job posting description from their web site and staple them together. I keep these in folders by location. This way when I do go for an interview, I have a hard copy of my research handy.

This chapter is about *expanding your initial list.* You probably have some of the company names and job descriptions already, and now you will need to build a comprehensive list. The length of this list is important and will keep you busy and motivated for a long time. You won't run out of options, as you will be moving through this list in a practiced and planned manner. You will need to go a step further and now go back to those sources and try to expand that list to include <u>any or all firms</u> located in that city/state (you can get this from a source such as Hoovers). You can also visit job boards for that city and see what jobs are posted and what companies are posting and add those companies to your list along with the job descriptions.

The goal here is now to expand and build a long (100 potential employers minimally in total) and comprehensive list of companies who might offer jobs in your field or in the job areas you identified by location. You can search in Hoovers by industry first for specific industries of interest, by location, and by other criterion such as size of company, or number of employees or HQ location. The minimum information retained should include the company name, address and what they do primarily out of that location (i.e. Headquarters, regional sales office, manufacturing facility). Hoovers and OneSource are both good sources for this information. But if you cannot afford to subscribe to Hoovers, if only just for a month or two, you will have to look in the Business White Pages on the internet or do searches through other sources such as the local business journals.

Now that you have a long (I'm suggesting 50-100 names per location) list of companies, by location of choice, you now go to each company's web site, FaceBook page and LinkedIn page to see what jobs are posted there. You can find this out in several ways:

- Their web site. The web site will have job postings for that company and location
- Their FaceBook and LinkedIn Sites. If you have set up a basic LinkedIn page for yourself, you can search the company by name and see what job postings they have. Many companies also have a FaceBook page and you might see job postings there. (For now, don't invite anyone to be your associate on LinkedIn or to be a FaceBook friend until this chapter is completed. This detail is covered in the next chapter as part of "applying for jobs".)
- Job Boards
    o Industry Specific Job Boards (Finjobs.com, salesjobs.com etc.)
    o Local Job Boards (i.e. Tampajobs.com etc.)
- Newspaper Ads

You might be very interested in a particular company but did not see any job ads that fit. This doesn't mean there are no jobs. It just means you might have to work a little harder to connect with that company and find a contact there or a recruiter who can help you.

After you have this comprehensive company list along with job descriptions, you might note any similarities in the job descriptions you found. Read them over. For example, you may be looking for accounting jobs but found a lot of financial analysis or Information Technology-type finance positions. If you can categorize these jobs descriptions into types, such as auditors, financial analysts, and sales of accounting software, this will help you in the resume preparation phase. The resume is going to be written with the type of job in mind. So jot down the categories you saw posted most often. Several resumes may be required with a different "twist" on your experience and education to fit the job descriptions by type. It also is helpful to recognize what jobs are posted and what jobs you thought about that you see posted less often or not posted at all. This doesn't mean these jobs don't exist; it may mean that they are offered to internal candidates or filled by references by employees. It's always best to focus your search on the areas that are the most in demand and make the other areas more secondary in your search.

Now that you have a long list of companies by location, along with the job descriptions available and posted at a particular company and location, and ranked in order of preference (job type or location), you are ready to start "preparing" to apply for jobs.

Planning Step 6: Have Job-Specific Resumes Prepared -

At this juncture in the book, you have spent a lot of time thinking and gathering information that will help you take pointed action in your job search. You have identified job types and descriptions, you have identified locations in priority order where you might want to live/work, have identified companies in these locations who might offer these jobs (and maintaining a list of publications/newspapers/business journals in these locations to continue reading to keep current on business news/activities and in case of new options that might come up), and have identified a list of people in these companies, or people who live in these communities who might be able to help you during your job search. Hopefully, in *talking* to people you have learned something about yourself and about the companies and the jobs available so you are more knowledgeable and have some inside information about what it takes to obtain an interview or a position at some of these companies.

Now that you have all of this information, you will need to prepare for the application process. In order to apply successfully for any job, you need to be prepared to fill out the job application and provide a resume
This can be a tedious process, often requiring repeating the same information. The resume needs to be accurate but can be formatted to use words, goals and descriptions that better fit the type of positions available for which you are applying .

Job Application Form

The job application is basically a repeat of the information on the resume (dates you were employed, the employer, the duration, and additionally, their address/contact name/phone number. It may also require your social security number and driver's license number. So what I would recommend is to put together "application information" on a separate set of documents and bring it with you, so you can be sure you fill out the application accurately if you are asked to do so. The information you will need is:

- Name, Addresses (past two or three), driver's license number, social security number,
- Dates and Names of education institutions you have attended, degrees you have been awarded and years in which they were awarded
- Any additional education (classes or certifications), any organizations where you are a member actively

- Dates (accurate month/year to month/year) of employment, employer name, address, phone and contact name (if you have someone there who can be reached)
  - Salary received while there
  - Job titles while there
- References, primarily business references that can vouch for you. Name, Title, Relationship to that person, and contact information. Better, bring several letters of recommendation, signed with the person's title and contact information.
- Information on US citizenship (green card etc) and Criminal record (be honest if you have any convictions or outstanding warrants)
- Other items specific to the job you are applying for at this firm
- Job title applying for
- Job skills (some people here include things like skilled with Microsoft Office including complex spreadsheets/Excel, other software products they have worked with, types of skills you bring to this job)
- Salary - Do not name a salary you expect, rather put "to be determined" or "negotiable". They may also ask what your salary was at prior positions. If they are the same position in the same industry, you can provide a total compensation dollar amount (includes bonus and other items). However, if the other jobs are not pertinent to this position, then leave it blank.

Some employers will not talk to you UNTIL you have filled out the application, whereas others will ask you to fill it out only after the first interview or just before the interview. Many companies are required to validate US citizenship and ensure someone does not have a criminal record before even considering them for a position. If you are not a legal US Citizen or if you have any type of criminal record, unfortunately, you may not proceed much further in the job application process at that firm.

Preparing for a Background Check and Credit Check

Employers will often follow up on past jobs and additionally, may run a criminal background check and a credit check. They typically run this level of checks after they have decided to offer you a job and need to make sure you "pass" before a formal job offer is extended. The credit check is primarily to identify if you have financial problems or issues paying bills. This may seem irrelevant to job performance in many jobs. But in some companies, they have researched and found that people who have past financial problems are "distracted" and possibly might be more apt to do something dishonest then someone who has pristine credit. If you are young, you might not have bad credit but may find that you have no credit history. It's best to put the car loan, insurance, and a credit card in your own name, and then make sure you pay off the bills in full each month, for one year before the job application process begins.

You can and should go to the credit bureaus (pick one of the three: Experian, TransUnion or Equifax) and go directly to their web site and pull a free "credit report". Each bureau is required to give you one free report per year, and there is no payment required to get it. They will however, offer to provide monitoring or other services for a fee. Skip that for now, you are simply ascertaining that your credit is clean and nothing negative should be on it. What you will see is anyone who tried to offer you credit in the past reached out to get information about you from the credit bureau (this shows up on your report). If you don't want these firms contacting you (banks, insurance companies, credit card companies, etc) then make sure you let the credit bureau know you do not want anyone accessing your credit (there is a place to do this online on their site, or call them). You may also have to pay something to get a credit score or FICO as it's known. You can do that if you want a copy of the score for your records. Otherwise, you can just check the report to make sure it's clean and accurate. You should see any credit cards and total line of credit available, any balances outstanding, any loans or other debts and the payment status. If you see ANY credit cards or other items that raise a red flag, this is the time to clean them up. Sometimes, people might use your identity to apply for loans or credit cards. If you see something like this you will need to notify the bureau that fraud has been committed. Overall, you should see a clean report with some credit (one card or whatever you have) and a solid payment record.

Additionally, you want to be sure to clear up any old issues with outstanding traffic tickets or issues with your driving record. This may all seem to have nothing to do with job hunting but in fact, if the decision comes down to two candidates and one has a good solid credit record with no outstanding issues and the other has a spotty record, the one with the spotty record may not get hired.

Another piece of information on the job application is going to be the references, both personal and business. In my opinion, personal references aren't worth much unless the person is well known in the business community (an executive level or president of a charity, large company or other institution whose name will be recognized) or is a person others value such as a teacher, coach or college professor or dean. An personal reference with no relevance or title will usually never be called. So try to identify personal references from influential people only.

Preparing Your Resume

A professional resume contains a snapshot of information about who you are and how/why you might fit a company culture and job description. Many companies use computers to screen resumes submitted by strangers (i.e. not provided through an internal reference process) and look for specific backgrounds, past employers, and key words. That is why a resume is not a onetime product you produce and use for every job submission; rather, it's a synopsis of your fit for a particular company and position. If an employer has to "search" your resume for any match of information, then it's probable there won't be a match and you will be eliminated before you even set foot in the door or speak to anyone at that company.

There are various resume formats where information is ordered in such a way as to highlight what is best about you first, followed by less relevant information. Many students with little experience list education first, followed by jobs/internships, then by personal interests such as clubs/hobbies/etc., followed by references. Most people list "available upon request" regarding references. This format is NOT the preferred format for the successful job search. People are not interested in hiring someone who has no experience and has little to offer but personal hobbies. The resume needs to represent you as a professional, not a student, and should represent the type of jobs you want and are suited for, your motivational level, your best skills, your experience, and your goals. As a result, the resume format I recommend in this order is:

- Career Goal
- Career Experience summarizing type of experience, duration of total experience, and accomplishments.
- Education (Including GPA and achievements that are noteworthy). This may also include honor society and honor fraternities, international education programs, etc.
- Other Achievements and education (certifications and experience working with software or within specific industries or different business types, and rewards/recognition received outside of school. Technology certifications are important such as proficiency with Microsoft products such as Word and Excel, for example. Also, state experience using major systems and applications that are installed in companies where you worked (Retail, Accounting, Inventory, and ERP systems specifically). These can include product names of business intelligence software, retail, hospital or niche systems for any industry etc. specifically if they apply to your industry or job search).
- Professional references only. State either a summary of references by company name and person name/title or actually provide 3-4 reference letters.

- Other: This is where you can identify a willingness to relocate to a city or area of the country. State hobbies and interests that could be an asset to acquiring a job.

Verbiage to avoid on a resume is using words that are too "trite" i.e. good, best, experience, problem-solving, team-player, proactive, objective, detail oriented, reliable, and responsible. Rather use a thesaurus to determine some replacement words that connote a stronger message and describe what you did or how you did something, and what you accomplished for the company, not just describing personality traits.

Ideas on words you could use to replace trite words (trite words in parenthesis):
- Use "Excelled at" rather than (good/best),
- "Awarded or received awards/recognition for" (experience),
- "Analyzed data" (problem solving),
- "Led a team" or "selected as a team lead" or "worked in a team setting to___" and state specifically what you did__(team-player),
- "Anticipated a requirement and delivered a solution" (pro-active),
- "Embraced change" (objective),
- "Used/Analyzed X data sources to determine_____" again, state specifically what you determined____(detail oriented),
- "Delivered on time/on budget" (reliable),
- "Leadership roles in___", state specifically what you led and why it was important to the company (responsible for).

"References available by request" and "salary negotiable" are just space takers. These are common sense items. As mentioned, putting together a few reference letters in the set with your resume and bringing along a copy so the references are in their face is more effective then stating "upon request". If you are sending the resume only with a cover letter, you can highlight on the resume under references, the name and title of the persons who wrote you a reference letter. The other benefit of a reference letter, it often removes the need to contact anyone; after all, they provided their opinion in the letter. As already mentioned, any reference should be a person whose name and title will be recognized or is an authority figure (Dean of a school, Teachers, Executives that are friends). Professional references can be co-workers, managers, but preferably executives who have worked with you.

"Salary negotiable" is empty language. The hiring company determines the salary range for the position and likely any negotiating will take place within that range, not within a range you set.

The resume should not exceed two pages no matter how much experience you have. If you have had a lot of jobs or changed jobs often over a period of time, it's better to summarize the job experience by type than it is to list a lot of jobs where you held the position two or three months or one or two years if you are older.

A good example was a construction manager who worked for me years ago, helping me to build my and a neighbor's home. He had worked 7 years for a large construction firm building subdivisions. He then started his own business building room additions and smaller projects for a year. The work wasn't steady, so he had a short stint with a larger firm again, only about 6 months, and then was laid off from that job. This obviously depleted his motivation greatly. He had a wife and children plus some minor health problems. He got another construction supervisor position with a smaller construction firm and was laid off from there after a few months due to health issues (heart problems due to stress). He then did odd jobs for about a year or two, working as a contractor for one firm while managing a few small construction projects (room additions, new driveways, new pools etc) on the side. Finally, he got two jobs building homes as a construction manager and managed those jobs for a year. One of these was mine. He now told me, he preferred to go back and work for a larger firm. He wanted to get back to the type of work he had done for 7 years, supervising larger projects. However, he felt his short stints and health issues would bite him and wasn't sure how to land this type of position permanently. He asked if I'd look over his resume and possibly improve it.

The resume read just like the above list. I looked it over (3 pages long) and saw a running list of jobs of all types and duration, no specialization or career goals. It seemed he was just looking for any old job and didn't bring much to the table. His job descriptions were things like, built a room addition or supervised a new driveway replacement. Big deal!

The first thing I told him was to figure out where he really wanted to work. I wasn't well versed in the industry, but I suggested home builders who were larger and established in the area in and around our city. A few names popped into my head of national firms who were building in the area. He indicated yes these were the type of firms he wanted to work for. I then showed him how to look up the firms on line and search their job ads for positions available. I saw the websites had postings for people who could supervise construction of entire subdivisions or multiple houses, along with "assistant" supervisors who oversaw just a subset of the work. I copied these descriptions from two different firm's websites, and then proceeded to rewrite the resume. While I was rewriting the resume, I asked who he knew that might be working at these firms. He stated he didn't know anyone. Really? I found that hard to believe. I told him, call all the subcontractors you know and ask them if they know anyone working there. Call some old friends and ask them, find someone. Surely there is someone working there or working with these firms who you know. Sure enough, the framing company he worked with for years had been doing work for both of these firms. They knew the current supervisors and provided him this contact information and an introduction.

The resume was then rewritten in the format described in this chapter. The career objective matched the job positing titles and skills required. For example, Experienced Construction Supervisor searching for long term career opportunity with leading construction firm, where over 20 years managing construction efforts for homes, subdivisions, and home additions is required. Skilled in negotiating and managing contracts, maintaining strong relationships with multiple subcontractors and homeowners, and delivering work on time and on budget.

The remainder of the resume due to the large number of jobs he had held summarized the jobs into three categories. Large Subdivision Supervision Jobs, Supervision and Delivery of Home Improvement Projects, and Lead Contractor for Home Construction. I described in each category the total years of experience added together and what types of things he achieved in each. For Large Subdivisions, he supervised ALL daily activities on the job, including land preparation/surveys, foundation, framing, construction and finish work with over 30 contractors in a typical job. He retained positive relationships with all parties, resolved billing and quality issues, long term positive relationship with homeowners on warranty work.

For the Home Improvement Projects, he not only supervised all this work, he found and negotiated contracts with subcontractors and managed all the invoicing, collections and work scheduling for the entire jobs. He managed several jobs at one time and maintained the schedules for these jobs.

For the final position, Lead Contractor for the Home Construction, he did the same as above, including doing some of the work himself around carpentry and finish work. Finished the jobs on time and on budget. Owners highly satisfied (with owner's references available). As a result of this approach, he had only "three" job types, each with 5-10 years of experience. I tried to include words and activities that were listed as important in the job descriptions I had gathered from those two construction firm web sites.

At the bottom, I listed the professional certifications and organizations to which he belonged (was licensed carpenter and licensed construction supervisor with X certifications) and provided references and listed the subcontractors (by subcontractor name, not person name) who would be willing to provide a reference. He had a large number of past subcontractor contacts, so we picked only the local recognized names and put the company name, contact name, and years in business.

He got one of the jobs he applied for and I believe it was largely due to the personal introduction by the contractor and the resume that exactly called out his qualifications for that job. Of course, the interview counted for something. He was surprised he told me after, that they never asked him about why he left any of the jobs, and he realized it's because none of the jobs were listed. He was asked what firms he had worked for and he mentioned the two major firms where he had worked and his own business for 10 years as well. No further explanation was required. If he was asked how long he had been at any one firm, he could just say 1-10 years depending on the job duration. That implies he never left until the job was done.

The importance of the above story is that the effort to come up with some contacts, and a custom resume was one or two weeks of time. By taking the time to make sure he met the qualifications and having his contacts help him get the introduction, he placed himself squarely into the position as an "exact fit".

In the past (10-15 years or prior), the resume was provided in hard copy and along with a written letter. So the type of paper it was printed on and the format and quality of the letter that was written played a key role. Today, the paper portion is minimized and the letter ends up more often as an email introduction. You should however, print your resume on quality thick paper (any office supply store has it) preferably in a color other than white (light blue, off-white, gray are preferred) so that the resume stands out and provide a hard copy without being asked during the interview process. The way it looks and the quality of the paper will stand out and could make a positive impression. No need to do anything crazy with this process, such as spraying perfume on the resume or providing the resume with some type of gift or other memorable antic. These things make you seem desperate and frankly, I don't see them as overly professional.

Once you have written up your resume(s) for each type of job description, you can print them out to make sure they represent a positive well formatted impression on paper. You can also, once you have written up your sample resumes, have a few people look them over and provide input for improvement. Finally, if you are highly concerned that your resume could read better, you might go online and find a professional resume service, which for $50-300 will take what you have written and offer you a set of enhanced options, including optional formats to consider. This is a wise thing to do early in your career, as you have less experience and these people write professional resumes for a living.

Earlier in this chapter, you identified a list of job titles and descriptions that are of interest to you. If you put these into categories, you can now use these to create several resumes, using the same basic information on your experience and background but making some slight changes to the information so that it best presents you for the job type. Below is more detail on the resume sections and what they ought to contain in the order that is important:

1. Career Goal
2. Career Experience
3. Education (Including GPA and achievements that are noteworthy).
4. Other Achievements and education (certifications/experience working with software or within specific industries or different business types, rewards/recognition received)
5. Professional references names/titles or better, attached to the resume.
6. Other—this is where you can list willingness to relocate or live in the Southeastern United States etc. People sometimes say something like "willing to relocate for the right opportunity" To me this is too vague, I would rather see, "willing to live and work anywhere in the Southeastern United States".

Career Goal

Career Goals are the first thing that is read by a recruiter or hiring manager who will first "skim" the resume for a job match. The Career goal should not be a canned meaningless statement such as "A professional position where leveraging accounting and financial analysis skills and leveraging strong communication capabilities are required." More likely this type of goal will be skimmed and excused as it says nothing about the person applying or what they really want or expect. The goal should represent what type of job you want that fits your skills, period. Nothing else. However, if creatively written, the type of job that fits your skills IS the job they are hiring for. So you will need two things to create this goal, first, you will need the job description for the position types or titles (you already have the job descriptions into categories by type) and you will need a list of your skills that fit those listed in the job description.

For example, the job description could say "Minimum of 10 years of experience selling and managing renewal software business in large fortune 500 accounts. This includes the following requirements

- Five years of sales experience
- Five years of management experience
- BA or BS in Marketing preferred, MBA a plus
- Demonstrated results having met or exceeded annual quotas
- Willing to work independently and a self starter.
- Experience selling technology products and services
- Proficient with Microsoft Excel , Word, PowerPoint
- Accurate Forecasting to annual quota required

So what is needed here is someone who has experience selling technology products or services to large companies, doesn't require a lot of supervision, and has some management experience (whatever that might mean) and successful track record forecasting and achieving their quota numbers.

Even if you don't have all the requirements for this job, if you at least can match to half of them, you might have a shot at the job. If you have no sales experience and no experience working with large firms or making a quota, you will likely NOT have a shot at this job so it's important to not waste time trying to obtain jobs where the fit is 25% or less of the required skills.

Additionally, there are certain skills that ALL employers want and expect today. Many employers would put a candidate with these skills at the top of the list. These skills are:

- Computer experience including: Data Analysis, working with specific systems and applications by name/brand, social media experience (beyond just using it), setting up twitter campaign or working on web marketing campaign), digital media, publishing, branding, and modern computer skills such as using spreadsheets for financial analysis or working on a current corporate system.

- Math and Science expertise (rarer to find people good at these topics, analytical type people)

- English/Journalism/Writing experience (Someone who is well read and can write eloquently).

- Well traveled, adventurer, hiking, mountain biking, safari, toured Europe or ___ country, speaks multiple foreign languages, attended a semester(s) in College overseas. (adventurous, willing to try new things).

- Athletic people who participated in a team sport or sports, run marathons, competed in Iron Man Events, etc. (Healthy lifestyle, goal oriented). These people communicate a higher energy and discipline level.

- Outside interests and activities including clubs, coaching, charity, church, etc. (not a workaholic) which shows balance.

So you might write a career goal for this job that says, "Experienced successful technology sales leader, looking for opportunities to manage a territory selling technology products and services to large customers, where independent self-motivated person can exceed annual quota".

If you view the above, it clearly says that you could fit this job description.

Career Experience

Experience can be listed as a chronological order (starting with most recent) of employers along with the jobs and activities and successes you had while at this firm. It could also be a summary of experience by skill types or titles and how much time and what skills you have achieved in each area. The way to present this depends on several factors. You might ask yourself these questions:

Have you worked for companies that are highly respected in your industry? If so, then the name recognition can give you some credibility. If however, you have worked for a lot of companies, only a few of which have recognized names, and many for short duration, you might consider the job title/skill type approach. An example of this was provided in the earlier section when describing the construction manager's resume. You can still provide some of these company names but your highlight won't be company, job title and duration, rather it will job title, companies (multiple), total years of experience (dates in a range) and then list the skills and accomplishments.

  o *Have you had the same type of job over and over again at numerous companies?* If so what is the job title and description, what did you achieve, how many years of experience would you say you have in this job area?
  o *Do you have little work experience (perhaps a recent graduate?).* If you have had internships at recognized companies, I would list the companies by name and the title and job tasks. I might skip the duration entirely. If you worked at jobs/companies that have little to do with the job for which you are applying, I would go with the work experience type (sales for example) then list what things you have done related to that field. Examples of types of work

experience that are needed in most jobs are sales, financial, management/leading teams, responsible for others, etc.

Follow this section about the Company/Title/Dates of Employment with a list of your achievements only. List notable achievements such as promotions, awards, overachievement of quota etc. Try to use words from the job ad specifically if at all possible.

Examples of each type, note in italics come directly from the job ad:

o By Company

XYX Technology Co, Senior Sales Manager, May 2000-Present
Sold Technology products including database and Business Intelligence to large companies including F 500 company ABC Corp.
Exceeded Annual quota 130% all years at company, attended Presidents Club and Regional Roundtable events by invitation only
Accurately forecasted using Microsoft Excel tools each quarter

o By Job type

Senior Sales Representative (Duration ie.2 years)
a) Managed a territory as a field sales representative, working with customers of all sizes including Fortune 500 companies in southeastern US.
b) Managed Territory development as self-starter and overachieved quota annually by 5-10% each year
c) Sold technology products including project management software to clients in the southeastern US.
d) List of company names you worked for during these two years.
Junior Recruiter (Dates)
a) Identified and recruited technology contractors for three client companies
b) Developed all business from scratch via own initiative
c) Highest producing salesperson in the company throughout tenure at company.
d) Names of Companies you worked for with this title)

Technology Internships (Dates)
Two years of intern experience in the technology industry working for Company A, Company B and Company C.
Types of work included Developing reports and spreadsheets using Microsoft Office tools, analysis of technology to use for account systems in XYZ industry.

As you might note, this "by company" person has spent a lot of time with one firm only but has a lot of the requirements of the job description. Person two, job type, probably doesn't have as much experience, a total of what appears to be about six years, but he/she has highlighted that they have done work that fits some of the requirements. The first title might have been two jobs, one year each, but they have not pointed that out. This is fine, but when they go to an interview, they might be asked to "step me through the resume and talk about your experience". They might then ask how long you stayed and why you left. We will cover these things in the interview skills, but it's critical to make sure you are not untruthful in your resume; rather a highlight of what you have done is more vague and doesn't call attention to a lot of job changes.

Education

Education may seem obvious, but most people primarily just want to know if you went to college, what your degree is in and any other training or certifications you might have relative to formal degrees. This section should be simple and to the point. Typically you will put the last education institute attended, any final degree you received, and the date you received it/graduated. IF your GPA is high, then put that as well only if you graduated five or less years ago. GPAs are less important once you have experience. Some people recommend you putting the total years you attended, but I personally do not feel this is required. Some people today finish their degrees over longer durations then 4 years, because in some states more classes or a fifth year for that degree is required, or they had to work or changed their major. These all seem to be personal reasons that don't matter. If you attended more than one university, it is ok to list that, if degrees were attained at each; however, if you went to a junior or local community college two years and received an AA then transferred to a major university, it is not necessary to put that level of detail unless your community college years obtained a degree that is in addition to your final degree. If you went on to graduate school but didn't finish, you might list that you are still completing that degree (list what that degree is going to be).

Example:
MBA (1 year, still completing degree in night school) University of X, Chicago Illinois, 2002
BS Mathematics, University of Y, Gainesville Florida, 2009. GPA 3.4.
High School, XYZ St. Louis Missouri, 2004. GPA 4.0 Summa cum Laude and Valedictorian, National Honor Society, graduated with honors, Varsity Football Captain.

If you want to list your high school, you can but it's not necessary, as to attend college requires a high school degree. However, if you graduated Summa Cum Laude or had a high GPA or other significant achievements, why not list them? You need to stand out academically, so it's good to do it any way you can. Also, the saying "it's a small world" is true, you might find that the interviewer grew up in St. Louis, knows your high school or attended the same college. This gives you something in common to share.

Achievements/Certifications

This section is for any achievements outside the degree. Examples are: President of your fraternity/sorority, recognition and rewards received during high school, college and thereafter (if not listed as part of your honors received in the education section). If you are a volunteer fireman, were in the military, or participated in any clubs or other affiliations that are nationally recognized, you might list these.
Professional References
Professional references are primarily people who could be used as a job reference and they should fall into any of three categories: people who are well known in the community/high level title, people who you worked for in the past and were your supervisor or have a supervisory type title from that company, or people who have worked WITH you in some capacity and have a notable title or authority. A peer reference is probably acceptable, but not of the same caliber as a supervisor.

These references can include people such as coaches, teachers, or in other positions of authority. Note that most people *will not call or email your references* without first letting you know they are doing it. As mentioned earlier, the reference letter provided at the interview might mean they never ask to call. However, it goes to credibility when the actual name and title and contact is listed rather than "available on request" and the person listed has a notable level of seniority. As mentioned earlier, it's best to bring 3-5 documented reference letters with you and provide them with the resume.

> *Reference List on the Resume, Example:*
> *John Doe, CEO of XYX Corp, St. Louis Missouri, optional email address or phone number of John.*
> *Susan Smith, Dean of Students, University of X, optional her email address or phone number.*
> *Stacy Jones, Director of Sales, Z Company, optional email address or phone number of Stacy.*

Other

List anything else of interest that might cement your relationship with anyone interviewing you for this job. This could be hobbies that might make you stand out in some way, i.e. Athletics (such as playing on a recreational sports team, running

Marathons/Triathlons (with some detail, such as completed over 50 Marathons or one of only 100 people in my age group to be selected to run the Chicago Marathon), Rock climbing (climbed the face of Mount Everest) for example. Sports or Physical fitness is important to mention because people who are physically fit and energetic are desired by many companies. If you don't have anything that interesting, don't list anything, however, I personally feel that these types of things just make the person more or less interesting. If all you can say is you like to work out and stay in good shape, I don't think that is a bad thing to mention. Do call out if you have some interesting or unique hobbies that could be a conversation starter or something they can remember that makes you stand out from the crowd. One person I knew listed "fartlekking" as a hobby and of course, this caused a stir and had many interviewers wondering what that was. It turns out it's a sprint type of running, and jogging combination. If your hobbies are reading, sleeping and knitting, or other mundane things, it's best not to put this type of information.

You might prepare 3-5 resumes, each targeting a specific type of job or that can be changed or modified to target a specific like-type description. A good example of someone who did this was a friend who was a programmer at a large defense firm, and he wanted to change into a job that got him out of the office more often. Call him *Scott*.

Scott liked meeting with people and leading a team. Two jobs we thought might fit his skills were a Systems Engineer (presales technical person) at a software firm with technical software products (like programming tools, engineering systems, defense based applications etc) or a technical sales job where you would be selling a highly technical product that served the defense industry or software development industry. We created two resumes, one for each role. Each had a different career goal and a slightly different twist on the job history section of his resume. We highlighted different skills and key words from job ads at companies we identified had the potential to hire someone in these roles. He ended up finding a job in his second choice location using this approach.

Another similar situation was a friend Mark, who was a CPA at a public accounting firm. He liked the work, but didn't want to stay in Public Accounting. So we identified two possible jobs for him, financial analyst (someone who uses the accounting financial systems to put together budgets, plans, and analyze financial information for a company), and secondarily, a salesperson who sells financial accounting systems. This is the exact same approach as taken for the programmer, the two resumes with the different career goals and slightly different job history descriptions highlighting the different skills and attainments targeted for financial analysis or for sales of accounting software. He got two job offers, one in each industry and ironically wasn't sure which one to take. He ended up calling The Psychic Hotline (not kidding) and asking the psychic on the other end which job to take. He laughs about this today, twenty-five years later after having a long and successful career selling financial and other software.

Finally, when preparing a resume you will need to use a thesaurus to find words that mean similar things to avoid redundancy. Try to avoid words that are over-used or have become clichés. Avoid common phrases that impart little detail and imply you follow directions rather than just think on your feet:

- "Experience working on or in"; instead, describe things you have accomplished or achievements.
- "Problem solving skills"; instead, describe challenges you faced and solutions you created to solve them.
- "Exceeded goals"; be specific: tell what the goals were and what did you do to exceed them.
- "Detail oriented"; instead describe projects that required a lot of analysis and data to be considered and the way the project was delivered.
- "Proactive"; instead say "demonstrated", "anticipated and addressed".
- "Works well on a team" or "team player"; describe situations where you worked on a team as a team lead or team member.
- "Conscientious" and "hard-worker"; instead say how you worked to beat a deadline or came in on a project under budget or ahead of expectations. State things you did that reflected your sense of responsibility.
- "Achieved the goals"; rather talk about where you went beyond meeting the goals and overachieved, over-delivered, and stood out from the crowd.

The final step in preparing to apply for a job is to work on transferring your resume highlights to a LinkedIn profile and prioritize your list of companies, jobs and descriptions into five lists, highest priority first. The profile on LinkedIn is primarily your resume on line. Make sure to set up the profile to check that you are interested in looking for jobs, which will open this resume up for review by recruiters and employers. You can highlight some of the skills from all of your resumes (two or three) that you have created so its comprehensive enough to cover the gambit of interests and experience.

Planning Step 7: Order the Priority of Your Search A, B, C, D, &E

Congratulations. You have made it to the final step in the preparation process. You now have:

- Job title list that fit your skills and interests, grouped into job title or type categories.
- Company names where you could apply for a job by location.
- Job descriptions/postings by company by location.
- Prepared material for your job application process such as company and contact research.
- Set up basic LinkedIn page with resume highlights and cleaned up your FaceBook page for a clean on-line presence.
- Created a list of contact names of people you know who work at companies where you might want to apply for a job.
- Created a few "sample" resumes around job description by category.

The final step in the planning process is prioritization. It's important to create a set of priorities for your application process around your preferences and your research. You can create the priority by job type, by location specifically, by highest probability of getting an interview (because you know someone at the company or have a contact), or by size/stability of company. It doesn't matter how you order your priorities, it's your plan. Based on your findings, you can organize your application process into plans A, B, C, D and E. Each plan should have a minimum of 30-100 companies (Depending on how many you have in total) with **A** being your first and top priority, **B** your next priority and so on. You might specifically note the companies that were hiring in your preferred job as a top priority along with places where you have a contact. It pays to strike while the iron is hot, and if you see a job that fits your skills, and a person you know who works there that will help you, it makes sense to put it at the top of your list.

When applying for jobs, you will start-by working through your **A** list. When you have completed that list, you will start on your **B** list and perform follow up activities on your **A** list. When you have exhausted your **A** and **B** lists, you will start on your **C** list. The purpose of this exercise is to make sure you cover ALL the companies on your lists, in priority order with highest desired outcome first. The other purpose is to avoid the trial and error application process. You have enough work to keep you busy for months, so you won't feel discouraged and run out of options as you move through the process.

Section 2: Action—TAKING ACTION

Now that you have a set of prioritized plan, it's time to take action. Taking action involves reaching out to contacts and applying for jobs at your **A** and **B** list companies and Job choices to start. This chapter identifies the MOST successful ways to win an interview for a job and then how to ace the interview and clinch the deal by receiving a job offer. This chapter also outlines the least successful approaches to the job application process and why you should avoid these approaches.

When you start this process, you will start with social media and linking to contacts, and then with the company names and jobs by location on your A list and then the B list and then do the follow up on these, before cracking your C list and so forth.

In many ways, this section is the hardest for people to follow because it means you have to do some difficult and uncomfortable things, like talking to people you don't really know, asking for help, talking about yourself and taking risks. It involves writing letters, making sure there are no mistakes and that you have communicated concisely. Your letters and resume(s) tell who you are and what you can offer a company. These things can be uncomfortable for many people. People are often not comfortable talking to strangers. Applying for a job is a "hat in hand" type of activity, and can feel like a pathetic thing that only a loser has to do. Everyone knows people who "knew someone", and/or got a job without a lot of effort. However, you should be *THANKFUL* you are not one of those people. The reason is that people who never have to do anything uncomfortable end up feeling that things will just go their way without effort and when things don't go their way one day, they often have difficulty handling these setbacks. I've personally observed these "winners" completely fall apart. Learn now how to get "uncomfortable" and you will gain skills and confidence that are invaluable in your life, job hunting and beyond. Humility is a great quality and companies want self-starters, people who will try things and who are not afraid to fail.

The best example I can give is a girl I know who had everything she tried out for or wanted come her way. "Sally" was smart and pretty. Whenever she tried out for anything, she made it on the first try. She had a lot of friends and boyfriends without trying. People she knew helped her to get into organizations, clubs, and the best classes. But then the inevitable happened, things didn't go Sally's way and no one was there to bail her out. She followed a boyfriend to a new town after college and took a low paying job for which she was overqualified. The boyfriend wasn't too happy to see her; it turns out, as he was enjoying his freedom. He treated her poorly and disrespectfully. Now she found herself alone, in a strange town, working at a job she didn't love and having lost what she thought was the love of her life. She became highly depressed and her health became poor. For a long time (years), she ended up doing nothing about her situation. She spent a lot of time dating men she didn't intend to marry or who wouldn't commit.

Years later, she learned that the boyfriend had gotten into some trouble with the law. So actually, had she been with him, she might have ended up in a bad situation. So it was a lucky strike that this relationship didn't work out. The real point here is a lack of resilience. Failure teaches resilience. There was no plan B, and no take charge attitude about her life. The depression and indecisiveness cost years of her life when she could have been achieving her full potential. Many years were wasted rather than taking some uncomfortable actions to make the changes she needed. She had not developed a resiliency and the attitude needed to recover from setbacks.

This is similar to what happens to many people who are fired, or lose their job due to attrition or who have stale skills. They don't do anything differently; they just feel bad for their bad luck and fail to learn from the experience. Another way to look at this is that the situation presents an opportunity to try something new. Bad things can happen to anyone, the key lesson here is having a plan B (C, D and E) so you can ensure you are able to move on to the next thing and not wallow in the past. It creates a "resilient" mind, a person who knows unexpected things can happen, and thinks, "Here is what I will do if things don't go my way. "

Contrast that to another story of a person who never got anything the first and often not the second try. In high school, "Jenny" tried out for the dance squad three times and made it finally the third time she tried. But only as an alternate. She showed up for every practice and asked for extra help, and in the end, she replaced a regular who didn't show up for practice and Jenny had proven her attitude and work ethic and improved enough to be a regular. Lesson 1, she was willing to keep trying and work harder. While in college Jenny didn't find out who her roommates were going to be for her senior year until June of the summer prior to the fall semester. All apartments were sold out and her new roommates wanted to live in a house. The roommates went home for the summer, leaving Jenny, who was living off campus in an apartment with bus service only, to figure out where they should live. Needless to say, there were not many options for housing but Jenny took a bus to campus and walked the streets around campus, for miles until she found a street with a "for rent" sign on a house. Lesson 2, planning ahead doesn't always work, but you do what it takes to get the job done. No one else was walking the streets looking for houses, only Jenny.

After college, Jenny got married. She decided she didn't like her field of study (teaching) and opted to apply for business jobs. She applied for jobs advertised in the newspaper and found one that required a teaching background. She had a company car, 50% more pay and a great new job. She had also gotten a second offer, but turned it down since this one seemed more lucrative. Then the third month into the job, Jenny found out they were laying off people, and that most of the new people were being let go. She knew the writing was on the wall, so she started looking for other jobs. She called back the other company who had expressed an interest in hiring her during her earlier search. She didn't have a lot of time to look around as she knew it was at most a week before a pink slip landed in her lap. As luck would have it, three months later, they had not yet found a person for the earlier job. She told the hiring manager she decided she wanted to take this position after all and landed the job. The day she was let go was a Thursday; Friday she had the new job offer.

The moral of the Jenny story, is that Jenny became resilient as a result of earlier failures. She knew she needed to move fast; be the early bird and take action. She quickly formulated a plan B or C, and didn't take rejection personally. She knew that things happen for a reason, though you often never know nor understand the reason they happen to you and not someone else. Her attitude was "Don't dwell on it, seize the day and take action, keep a positive attitude and look at the situation as an opportunity". She had to be decisive, no mulling things over for weeks on end or getting depressed. This can-do attitude came from so many setbacks. At the time these experiences were devastating, but Jenny recovered well from all of them. She couldn't afford to be out of work financially. Reflect back on your own failures and setbacks, and note how you found the strength to move forward and likely, things worked out ok in the end.

In getting uncomfortable in the job hunting process, I recommend you embrace this process with a positive attitude. It's a learning experience. You might get rejected, but that isn't the worst thing that can happen. The worst thing is to do nothing, to mope around and give up, and blame the tough market or lack of opportunity. I say "nonsense", where there is a will there is a way. Be resilient, and have a "can- do" attitude. Get up every day and decide to do what others aren't willing to do. Believe me; you will stand out from the crowd.

It helps to both set goals and measure yourself against them and to have a long list of prioritized companies and opportunities. This way, you don't run out of things to do and end up feeling like you are starting over on your search. It may take a few weeks or months to get through this long list you have built which will help to keep you motivated throughout this process.

In this section, you will be taking action by doing four primary things
- Getting Your Name Out There
- Social Networking
- Advertising yourself
- Reaching out to Others

Getting Your Name out There

Primarily, this means letting people know you are looking for a job, but specifically, letting them know exactly what jobs you are considering. This means a lot of communication with people you know and with people you meet through other sources, including social networking sites.

If you can now go back to a list of people who you do know personally, this is the time to contact them and let them know that you are starting to apply for jobs and would like to get their input on specific types of positions, at specific companies, in specific locations. You have previously asked people for advice and you might already have them thinking about helping you. Now you can see if they are willing to help you. They may be willing to forward your resume on to someone at their company, or at a friend or business contact's company to help identify if you are a fit for a position. Of course, with your custom letter and resume, you will look like more than a match.

Too many people go straight to social networking as the only way to connect with people (meaning using the FaceBook or LinkedIn sites primarily, or sending texts, or Instant Messages. These are good methods, but they do not replace a personal meeting or personal contact. *People who know you personally, have seen or spoken to you recently, are more likely to help you.* Time causes people to forget. In this case, absence does NOT make the heart grow fonder. One reason for isolating this topic into its own section, is to make sure that when we get to *Contact List* below, that you identify who on your contact list is a personal contact and make these people your highest priority.

Social Media

Social Media is an excellent way to market yourself to the outside world, and those seeking employees look more and more to Social Media than ever before. The two main Social Media sources are FaceBook and LinkedIn. LinkedIn is the professional networking site for people to connect with business associates. FaceBook is more of a Social site for friends to collaborate on personal information. Companies usually retain a presence on both sites, so it's critical to have a solid, clean presence on each. If you have a FaceBook page, you will need to make sure your pictures, groups and other associations are clean and provide a positive impression of you. This means removal of pictures where you are drinking or partying, removal of any sexually explicit photos, removal of postings or comments that could be misconstrued as unprofessional, removal of questionable groups or clubs. You might want to block any postings of "friends" who have a shady or promiscuous online presence as well. The purpose of this exercise is to present a clean image to the outside world. You can become a fan of some of the companies on you're A list to start on FaceBook. You can "link" to company related sites on LinkedIn.

LinkedIn is the more important of the two sources for job searches. This is where you update your profile if you created one earlier, to include your resume updates and job types of interest. You can open your profile to anyone who is looking to hire people for jobs. Make sure to check the setting to be able to view any profiles of people who looked at your profile. That way you can see if people are viewing it or not. You should then reach out and request to connect to many professional groups, companies you are interested in, and any of the personal contacts you earlier gathered earlier. You can request to connect to all the companies on your A and B list initially. You also should search for organizations or interest groups in your industry such as financial industry groups and alumni groups from your University. Link to your college career office. These groups often have recruiters associated with them and they will be looking for prospective employees on LinkedIn. If you see any job postings associated with the company, either on LinkedIn or from their website, search for recruiters for that company and request to connect or you can apply to jobs that are posted. You will notice that if you set up your profile to seek jobs, you will receive an email of "jobs that may be of interest to you" with an automated list of jobs that were posted in your location, and areas of interest. If anything, this could introduce you to new companies or opportunities you missed in your former research.

You will find this process to be very effective with connecting you to people who can advise you on employment with that company. Many companies hire their own recruiters rather than pay an independent recruiter. However, independent recruiters may know people at the company or have ideas for getting you in for an interview, so listen to everyone, but never bank on only one source (say a recruiter who wants you to be exclusive with them). You can search for independent recruiters by putting in searches such as "Atlanta recruiters for financial industry" or "XYZ Recruiter" and variants of this theme. Find these independents and connect to them. In your settings and profile, you can set up what types of people can see your profile and make sure anyone can connect to you, especially those who are looking to hire. By joining some groups, college graduates from XYZ University, or industry specific groups, you can connect with other like-minded people working in the same industry or career type.

You should never pay any recruiter a fee to find you a job. If you run into anyone who asks for an upfront payment or a fee if they find you a job, just decline. Companies who allow outside recruiters will pay a finder's fee directly to that firm for anyone they hire. There is no reason for you to pay a fee. Also beware of independent recruiters who were not hired by the company to find them employees. These people are trying to position themselves to receive a fee. Often, they can't get you in the door as the company already hired a recruiting firm or is using internal recruiters. The company may not want or be willing to pay a fee. The fee charged to the *employer only (not you)* can be 50%-100% of the first year's salary or something less. As a result, if you do identify the company that is hiring, it is better to connect with recruiters who are hired by or work for that firm. Usually they will have a lot of jobs posted for that firm not just one.

If anything, you can upgrade your LinkedIn account profile for a fee and for a duration of a few months so that you get additional information available to you and put your name on top of search results. Review what is offered and if it fits, it's worth the extra money for a short period of time.

Contact List

Now that you have made social media connections, specific to your A and B lists initially, you will need to take a second look at your contact list that we started and defined in step 4 in Foundation. This is the time when you now want to reach out and email or call anyone who you identified on your earlier list as having contacts at companies or working in industries where you have an interest.

Some of this should already have taken place during step 4, but now it's time to really reach out and ask people for how to get an interview at their company for a *specific position* preferably, you have identified and you think you might be a fit. You are looking for a job in the following fields or industries; or you are interested in certain types of companies and in locations that are identified; or you can be specific with asking, "What advice would you give me on who to contact for this position?" If you haven't yet asked for help, now you can ask.

To review the types of questions you should ask include

- Specific to this job description or these jobs, who could I contact directly to ensure I get a shot at an interview? Make the point you screened the description and feel you are a fit.
- What kinds of jobs are available at your company for someone with a _____background?
- Do you know who is responsible for hiring for these type of jobs?
- What are the open job requisitions posted internally?
- Who is the hiring manager for the job posted?
- Where are they hiring (location)?
- How long has the job been open (the more recent, the better)?
- What is the job description—what are the requirements for this position? Maybe they will send you the internal posting.
- Do you know anyone who currently has this job or is hiring for these types of jobs (even if it's not the same person who has the open opportunity), if so, they can ask their contact what type of candidates are of interest—does that person know the hiring manager and what do they know about the manager?
- Most important, will they submit your resume to the job openings posted or send it to someone internally on your behalf? If they get a fee, they might be willing to do it.

It's important to now be quiet and listen to the answer. If the person doesn't want to help you, he or she will say something short and vague and exit quickly. If they do want to help you, listen to what they have to say, ask them how they got the job they have, what are some reasons they feel they have been successful there, and so forth. You will learn about the type of people they hire, the way people find jobs there and once there, what they had to do to be successful.

You will also want to link to these people through your social network connections if you haven't already. If you get a name or two at the company, view their linked in profile. You can try to link with them but if they don't know you, they probably won't respond. You can at least learn about the person and their background. If you do invite them to link, LinkedIn allows you to request to link via email, and it's an online email from the site. You can write in the email that you have spoken to person X and reviewed this open job position (reference the position number or title) and feel you are a fit for the position and would like to connect. Include your phone number in the email.

One benefit of these social networks is they often identify other people connected to people you know. Take a look at the other people, and if they seem to be people who can help you find a job, jot down their name and title and evaluate their profile. Request to link to them or friend them only sparingly, as most people will not accept an invitation from someone they do not know. By looking at their profile you can see what job they do and role/title in the company, past companies they worked for and any common interests and hobbies. It will help you see the kind of background/degree people have in that company. It is a matter of building up a knowledge base about the companies you are interested in and their employees.

You now should be ready to start the job application process. You have a list of companies and jobs that were posted on the websites/job boards/or were shared by your contacts. You have access to the company information and key contacts from Hoovers or OneSource or better from your own personal contacts. You have social media access where you can search for the company name and "friend" the companies and "linked in" to the company and to anyone searched as a XYZ (Company Name), Recruiter (Title). This is the key information you need, along with your ABCDE list of priorities.

Application process

It's finally time to start applying for jobs. The application process involves a fair amount of work for each opportunity. Most people will do a minimum amount of work: just sending a canned resume and cover letter via a job board or posting. The letters and resumes sent this way represent a generic set of information, and end up being sorted by a computer. The computer is going to get rid of anyone who applies who does not meet the minimum requirements of the company. These criteria might include:

- Lack of requisite experience (number of years or type of experience they are looking for).
- Lack of key words meeting their job posting requirements.
- Lack of education or degree they require or other criterion (such as GPA -- believe it or not, one company stated they would accept no applications where the College GPA was lower than 3.4, even if the person had 10 years of experience!).
- Poor resume or letter quality (misspelled words or poor grammar).
- Location: Person may not live in the location where the job is offered.

If the resume passes the screening process of the computer, it will land on a recruiter's desk, who will start sifting and sorting through the stack. These remaining resumes will end up in two piles, one for those who may receive a phone call or email from the recruiter or request for additional information, and one for those with lower probability who would only be called as last resort. The rest will be discarded. Likely these latter "last resort" resumes would be those who don't have enough experience, have long breaks in employment, or have perhaps changed jobs every few years, or worked at companies who are unknown or less desirable.

Should you be one of the lucky ones who ends up in the stack of possibilities you may get a call or email from the recruiter. They may ask for more information or request a quick call with you. They might have a few questions that are pre-set to screen out people and from there, will weed out those who can't answer succinctly, have poor communication skills, or don't meet the expected answer criterion. As mentioned earlier, *if you do not state clearly what you want to do in your career, and it's not the job they are searching for, then you will not get a call back*. People who know what they want, get what they want. So please keep that straight in your mind before you respond to calls or emails. If you do get a call out of the blue, you might state you are tied up and ask to schedule a time to call them back. That will give you the time you need to think about what to say.

There are even those who direct you to a website to take a survey that determines if psychologically you fit into their culture or meet their behavioral expectations. These surveys are created by psychologists to frame up a series of behaviors and personality types that do best in this position. Some of these behaviors listed are quite repetitive; i.e. a similar behavior but using a different word to describe it. There are generally four types of people and there are certain behaviors that fit each type. There is no "right" type of person in general, some jobs gravitate more to one type versus another. These four "types" have been named many things, but they fall under Driver types, Analytic types, Amiable types and Expressive types. Everyone has some of the qualities of multiple types, but generally fall mostly in one category or another. Below are some examples of the behaviors common to one type or another.

Driver Type of Person:
- Impatient
- Organized
- Steps into Leadership roles, can lead a discussion and coordinate a group of people towards a common goal
- Appears confident and self-assured
- Goal oriented
- Will jump in and summarize the points or purpose of a discussion.
- Clear communicator

Analytical Type of Person:
- Detail oriented
- Thinks things through, step by step
- Quieter in a group, will want to go back and review topics already discussed.
- Organized
- Patient
- Not emotionally expressive, keeps feelings to themselves

Amiable/Easy-Going Type of Person
- Easy going, can be shy
- Gets along with everyone
- Collaborator
- Works well in a team
- Decisions are made after seeking input from others
- Agreeable

- Indecisive

Expressive/Outgoing Type of Person:
- Verbose and talkative
- Funny and interesting
- Likes to tell stories
- Veers off topic to explain and elaborates with personal stories
- Likes to be center of attention
- Outgoing
- Gets along with many types of people
- Impatient, bored easily.

This is only representative of some of the common behaviors of these types. But once you understand these types, not only can you understand your style, but more importantly, *you can better recognize and accommodate the style of others.* People see you not as *you are* but as *they are.* So an expressive person might annoy an analytic person, because they seem to chatter relentlessly. The analytic person might annoy the driver, because he has moved past a topic that the analytic doesn't feel was adequately reviewed. The amiable can't seem to make a decision without asking others what they think, and the driver is ready to end the meeting already. If you can adjust your style somewhat for the person type you are dealing with in any meeting, you will have a more successful connection with that person.

Different types of jobs are more suited to different types of personalities. Sales people can be expressive or drivers or both. Managers are often drivers. Analytics are often math and science oriented people such as Engineers, Software Developers or Financial Auditors. Analytics make good team members and can be good managers for teams with long projects or where collaboration is a critical factor in the job. So really, there is no right type, just know what you are and understand that some jobs may require a different type of person. So the psychological tests are often developed to sort out certain types of people who they have researched to suit their company culture or job types.

Finally, only a small percentage (under 5%) will ever get to an in-person interview. The in-person interview might be with a recruiter or with a hiring manger. Then if you pass that meeting, you might get interviewed often by peers and/or by the hiring manager and their bosses. Then the last step is to pass all the background checks. Only one person gets hired.

Seems impossible? That is why the blind submission is almost always a complete waste of time. But add this final element. While you are applying on line, being screened out by recruiters and others, someone else is getting a personal reference and introduction to the hiring manager, meeting and interviewing and providing the company with a viable option for filling the opening. This person has a head start, even if not a perfect fit, they come with an employee reference. They have already completed several of the interview steps.

Many companies are required to interview multiple people for a position, but normally, having at least two qualified candidates is acceptable. So knowing that the two are not likely to come from the resume submission process as described above, how do you now feel about your odds of employment using this approach?

The application process requires a plan and a process. The plan you have already; contacts, company names, job postings/descriptions, recruiter or other names of people you don't know (from Hoovers, Social Networks, and other sources such as articles in your business journals and newspapers). You also have some priorities of your first and second choices (**A** and **B** lists), followed by three more lists (**C,D,E**). So instead of the blasting of resumes, you are going to start a pointed campaign to obtain employment at a company in the following order.

Starting with your **A** list, for every company and job opportunity and contact on you're **A** list, you will be contacting companies and people in the following priority order (with 1 being the best way and 5 the least attractive way to contact them):

1) **Personal Introduction to a hiring manager from someone you know.** (email is the norm)
   Or Personal submission of your resume to a job opening at that company, directly to the recruiter or hiring manager through a personal contact introduction preferably.

2) **Personal letter with your resume** (email is fine or US Mail is ok if there is no email option) to a contact at the company who you have identified as the job contact or recruiter contact for the job description that fits. Its best to have reached out to them and let them know your sending this resume.

3) **Email to recruiting contacts you identified through social networking for that company**
   a. Specific to a job posting

b. Specific to a type of job you are interested in
c. General—seeking to identify jobs for the following areas....

4) **Email or personal letter to a key contact at the company, not someone you know,** someone whose name shows up as a recruiter or key executive in the area to which you are applying—i.e. Sales jobs, VP Sales, Regional Sales Manager Northeast, etc. –Accounting Jobs, Partner at Location you are applying, Controller or CFO, etc.

5) **Blind submission**
a. Blind Submission to web site job posting on the company's website.
b. Blind submission to job posting on industry job board specific to your industry where
   you have the most experience or a degree.
c. Blind submission to a job board posting—should be and can be done at same time as item 4 only.

Below is more detail on how to do each of these things. The idea is to contact all of your **A** list then your **B** list using the above method's with item 1 being the best way all the way down to item 5 as a last resort. When you start on your **B** list, you at the same time, do follow-up work for you're **A** list.

Priority Steps for Getting an Interview: More tips for each step to follow.

1) **Personal Introduction to a hiring manager from someone you know.** (email is the norm) Or Personal submission of your resume to a job opening at that company, directly to the recruiter or hiring manager and most likely through a contact you made.

To get a personal introduction to a hiring manager, you will need to know someone who can and will be willing to provide that introduction. This person more than likely comes from that list of contacts and people you already have on your list. This would be perhaps the same person(s) who you spoke to about opportunities at their company, and they might have shared a job posting and offered to help you with the submission. *Ideally, you want this person to send your resume directly to the hiring manager, not to just the recruiter or HR person listed.* If the resume can be sent with a personal reference then that is best. If not, just sending it and having the person state that you are highly interested in this position with their company is a good start. Make sure you get the <u>hiring manager name, title, and email and phone number</u> if possible so you can follow up. If you do get an interview, the polite thing to do is to call or email the contact and thank them for their assistance and tell them you got the interview or not. Remember, some companies pay their employees if a referral is hired. So this is more than just a polite thing to do.

If you do not have anyone at the company whom you know, but you do have a job posting and contact name at the company, you can submit your resume directly to the contact (usually a recruiter but sometimes the hiring manager). If you know someone who works there who will be a reference for you, you might mention their name in the cover letter.

The cover letter is generally provided as a formal letter to present yourself and your resume to the employer/recruiter or hiring manager. You provide that along with the resume.

2) Personal letter with your resume

Email is fine or U.S. Mail is ok if there is no email option then to a contact at the company who you have identified as the job contact or recruiter contact for the job description that fits.

The format for a personal letter is formal and to the point. You can search on-line for *business letter* formats so as to address the letter properly. The letter is not conversational or slangy; it's not too formal so as to be stilted. I suggest a format of the following:

Example Letter Format:
Dear _____: (use the name—as a rule I say it's always better to err on Mr. Smith or Ms. Jones. I don't use the first name unless I have spoken on the phone to the person first).
Paragraph 1—Why am I writing?
Paragraph 2—Why would you want to consider me for this position?
Paragraph 3-Thank you and how to contact me.

It is helpful to create a few different letter formats from which you can cut and paste to customize. This way you will be sure to not misspell or leave out any details required.

Sample Cover Letter for Paragraph 1: Who are you and why are you writing?

I am responding to the opportunity for a __JOB TITLE__ *that I saw on* _____*(Source: A person name you know in the industry or at the company, LinkedIn or newspaper or company website). I am highly interested in this position because not only do my skills of* _____,_____, *and* _ _____*(take these skills right from the ad) closely match the requirements for this position, but I feel that I can be an asset to* _____*(Organization name).*

Example Paragraph 2: How will you be an asset to the company? Say something about the company that you could only know if you read their financials, annual report or articles about them.

I understand that _____*(Organization name) is expanding into the Southeastern United States and intends to grow the business over the next three years by 50%. One of my strengths is my ability to identify new client business and then drive business to closure. For example, I did this at* _____*when I* _____ *(or optionally, state exact contributions you made at another firm or firms, such as "I grew our client base by 100% in only two years").*

Talk specifically about how you would be an asset to the company by telling them something about yourself that is RELEVANT to the job posting. You want to talk about things you have done that contributed to other businesses that are direct measurable outcomes that this company would want for this position. (i.e. if its sales it might be quota overachievement, or development of new business. If its financial analysis, it might be identified trends that helped drive adoption of new approaches saving the company over $3 mil per year).

Sample Statement: *"Having worked in the financial industry for twenty years, I've had the opportunity to work on many projects and clients. My strength has been that I have been continuously recognized for the highest client satisfaction, and grew the base of business from my clients by 30% annually."*

Par 3: Thanks and how to contact me. Thank you for your time and consideration. I look forward to speaking with your personally. Please feel free to contact me at _____*. (you can also state you will follow up in the next two weeks, and then do it.)*

     Sincerely or Best Regards or Respectfully,
     Your Name

3) Email to recruiting contacts you identified through social networking for that company

As mentioned earlier, you can do a search on LinkedIn that says "company name, recruiter" and a list of recruiters may show up. Looking up the company name may yield a list of people who included company employees who are recruiters. Look for recruiters who work for that company. Many have a title that identifies the type of jobs they search for and the location of the country. Reach out and ask to link to these people who fit your profile. They may link back to you or not. But chances are, they will view your profile and you can identify people who have viewed your profile on your LinkedIn main page. If someone viewed your profile, that company may be hiring.

You should wait a few days and see if these people respond and link to you. If they do not, then you might send them an email from their LinkedIn profile. Let them know you are interested in a particular job type or title. Ask for some time to obtain information on how to pursue such an opportunity. They may not respond. If they do not, it's likely they viewed your profile online and do not feel there is any fit. If you believe you do have a fit with a specific job posting, then the next step is to search out the person's company email. This can be as easy as going to Hoovers and looking at the emails of executive names, some are always posted and use that format to reach out to them via email or pick up the phone and call them. Their number should also be on Hoovers, or the general number of the company. If you have tried all of these approaches, and there is no response, give it time. In the meantime you can always apply for the job online via LinkedIn or direct from the company website. This is really a blind submission so it is not the preferred approach. However, direct to the website is better than a job board, because it shows you are interested in this company.

4) Email or Personal Letter to someone at the company.

This is not someone you know, but someone whose name shows up as a recruiter or key executive in the area to which you are applying—i.e. Sales jobs, VP Sales, Regional Sales Manager Northeast, etc. –Accounting Jobs, Partner at Location you are applying, Controller or CFO, etc. Generally if you have tried the prior step, your other recourse is to reach out to the Highest Level Executive who might be hiring for this position. Usually a department manager is a good contact or title of Vice President. You can obtain this information on the website, Hoovers, or even on LinkedIn via the search capability. If you use this approach, you can use email, or you can call, but be aware that most likely, the person will either:

    a. Respond personally, let you know who you should contact.
    b. Ignore your email and nothing happens with it, or tell you not to contact them again

c. Forward it to someone who you should contact or who will contact you.

d. If it's a phone call, may have their administrative assistant screen you out. If you do get the assistant, you can ask him/her who you should talk to about this position. Be specific on the position of interest. She may give you a name or forward you on to this person via internal phone system. This is good as the call comes from an employee desk rather than from the outside.

With a), the person was told that you had a personal reference. With a), when you reach out to the person, via email or phone, you can reference that _____recommended you to contact him or her. This implies you know the person so you will be able to have a conversation about your interest in the company and a particular position. With c), the person who receives this forwarded note will quickly ascertain that you don't know the executive in question, so you can't imply you do. They might ask you how you know this person. You can state they are in your LinkedIn Network or were identified as the decision maker for this position. But you must follow-up and set up a time to talk over the phone or in person. It's important to speak directly to this person. They may ask for your resume to be sent and if you do that, they might eliminate you from consideration as it doesn't fit current job criterion. If b) happens, let it go. That doesn't mean you should give up, you need to find another contact at the company who will talk to you about a position you are interested in.

5) Blind submission

Blind submission is really a last resort, yet most people use this for almost all their applications. Most of the time, blind resume submission to a website posting only results in what was described earlier, and a machine short-lists people who most fit the requirements and likely it won't be you. One kind of blind submission is to make yours more personal. You might create a custom letter and mail it with your resume, along with the online submission. It might make you stand out. If you print your resume on fine-grain paper and write a very professional cover letter, it may get a second look. It's worth a try. It is better to address your letter to the Department Head by name than to just a general person who is a recruiter or Human Resources name.

Finally, if you actually had a name of a person you contacted in this process for a job opportunity,
attempt to make a note of that date and then a week later, go back and do some type of follow-up,

phone call, and an email asking if the application was received. Do this every week until you hear back. This shows persistence which will impress people that you are really interested.

Once you have completed this process for your **A** list, you will repeat it again for your **B, C, D** and **E** lists. Follow-up for each submission should be scheduled 3 days to a week after submission (depending on if Its email or U.S. Mail). So each week, you will have a primary set of job applications and a follow up set of activities. Once you complete these for you're **A** list, you move to your **B** list with the same procedures. With this approach, you will not run out of actions to take for a long time.

Setting, Measuring, and Attaining Goals

Plans have been made, first steps executed, and now it is time for action and assessment. We have so far planned on how to find a job. We have a set of priority places to work, job types we want and locations where we want to live. We also have a solid list of contacts from companies we are interested in, people we know, and contacts we identified online. We have a few good resumes and sample letters of introduction prepared. We know what to do, how to reach out and hopefully if we are moving through our A, B, then C, D, E priority lists, with follow up activities along the way, and we are on our way to lining up some interviews.

The hardest part of this process is the taking action part and doing it in an organized and methodical way. It may seem tedious, but it's no different than digging a ditch, one shovel at a time. A lot of us are good at a scientific set of steps to follow. The different ingredient here is that it takes guts and motivation to keep plugging away at the action items required to secure meetings, interviews and contacts. It takes tenacity to move through your lists and continue this process. You need to make sure you are ready because you will be busy!

The best way to get that motivation and keep it is to measure your success initially as you are going through the process of applying successfully. Set goals for yourself daily and weekly. You might decide that every day early in the morning, from 7 am to 11 pm, you will contact 10-15 of your priority opportunities or companies. You will also go back to the prior week and identify the companies you contacted that same day the prior week and do a follow-up phone call or email. At the end of each week, you should go back and measure how you are doing. One way to do this is to write the names of the companies/jobs you applied for on a daily calendar and keep a list for every day of the week. That way, you can see, "wow, I'm really knocking these out, last week I did 45 applications and 25 follow-ups".

The follow-up is just as important as the application, following up the week after shows you are persistent and truly interested. Following-up means an email or phone call to the contact to ensure they received your resume and letter and asking them what the next steps will be. If you don't hear back, put them down for the next week to follow up again.

Every three weeks or so you might have to take a look at what resulting interviews or responses you got from this effort. If you received no response then you might spend some time searching for another name at that company to contact about the position. Sometimes the second name will yield better results than the first contact you had. Even a negative response isn't bad, if you receive a response directly from someone saying that the position isn't a fit, you might use that opportunity to let them know what type of positions you are looking for and ask for advice on what type of jobs that company offers that could be a fit. It might open up a door for you.

You should file copies of all your emails and letters and responses. You can do this on your computer so that you keep an electronic copy of every communication you sent or received. You want to do this so you know which resume and letter you sent them, and make sure that your messaging in any follow-up and any interview will match-up with what you stated in your letter and types of skills in your resume.

In the end, a methodical approach with follow-up will yield interviews and opportunities. Now it's up to you to ace the interview and make sure the job is awarded to you rather than someone else.

Section 3: Getting the Interview

Some things covered in this chapter will include: What to know about Interviewing including the types of interviews, questions and topics to expect to cover during the interview tips to make you more successful in this set of communications; touchy subjects like compensation and other payment discussions; following up after the interview; getting a job "offer"; and handling rejection.

What to Know About Interviewing

Interviews come in many formats, they are not just in person. Today people might interview you in the following manner:

- First, through receiving your online or paper resume,
- Second, over the phone using a company or outside recruiter to screen candidates,
- Third, in person with the recruiter or hiring first level manager, and
- Finally, with other team members of that manager. Team members are upper management or executive levels in the reporting chain, peers or other managers on same tier as hiring manager, and/or employees who might be your peers.

We have covered the paper format, which is the preparation of the application, letter and resume, to
highlight your fit for the job description and company. The remainder of this chapter covers the
interviews where you are speaking with someone, a recruiter or manager or executive or peer. The discussion type varies depending on the level of person. If you can research the person at all, find out something about them on-line, such as "googling" them, looking them up on LinkedIn or FaceBook, you can have some information about the person professionally and possibly, personally. It can help get a feel for the person you are going to be talking with. Typically, the focus at each level is different, so the expectations might be:

Recruiter/Phone

This person's goal is to screen employees for hire. Mostly, these interviews take place over the phone rather than in person. If the person is an outside recruiter, they were hired by the company to perform this task. If they are an employee, they are primarily responsible for the same thing, however, they are paid a salary and likely not paid a fee for each employee they find who is actually hired. This second type (or fee paid by employer for each person found and hired) can create an incentive for the recruiter to present more candidates even if they are not highly qualified. You can find out if the recruiter is one type or the other typically by their email address. The outside recruiter might be interested in keeping your information for other positions, which is a useful thing. Keeping an open line of communication with all outside recruiters who reach out to you is a good idea for future job searches.

A recruiter will likely have specific skills they have been told to search for. The key words on your resume have caught their eye, however, this is where they will ascertain if you represent yourself accurately. They might dig into your job experience, your skills and their match to the role, and your flexibility (i.e. not having specific work hours, travel limits, or other demands that would limit your ability to do the job.). They will also be looking at your communication skills. Can you speak well, clearly and are you approachable in conversation.

Recruiters can answer questions about the job and company that might be useful in the face-to-face
interviews later, so it's best not to view this interview as something to get through so you get to the real decision maker. Rather, view this person as a resource who can tell you more about the company, culture, actual job activities, and give you tips on how to get hired. This is where a list of questions specifically for this level of interview should be drawn up. For example you might ask:

- What type of person have you typically hired for this role (i.e. what is their background, what about them has made them someone you want to hire?)
- What type of person succeeds at this job longer term (i.e. What skills did they see in hiring that worked out well for the employees longer term success).
- When you find someone who doesn't get hired, or doesn't work out, is the reason typically that they don't fit this company, culture or job, what are the top few things you see in these candidates that indicate a lack of fit? (i.e. Was it their personality, their job skills, their inflexibility, what mattered to the company in the rejection of that candidate).
- If they indicate they plan to get you an interview with the hiring manager, ask them if they can give you a little information about the person, i.e. how long has he/she been at the firm? What are the top 3-4 things that really leap out at this person as important?
- Ask the interviewer/recruiter about the next person you will be talking to, such as how long they have been at the company, how long in this role, and what type of people and backgrounds are they looking to hire.

Hiring Manager/Phone or in Person.

Sometimes the next step is to talk to the hiring manager. Normally the recruiter will set this up for you, and it could be over the phone if the person is remote, and will be followed by in person if they are interested and you both agree to proceed to the next step. Typically, you have done some homework on the hiring manager, perhaps you asked the recruiter about this person (How long have they been with the company, what type of background or skills are important to them, how long have they been looking for someone?). You can also look them up on Linked-in and see if there are any common contacts or other interesting facts you can glean about the person. For this type of phone interview, its best to prepare by having a few points you want to make (3-5) and these points can be about your fit for the job, your interest in the job, and possibly, your willingness to embrace change/flexibility. The idea being, if the interviewer leaves this call, what should they remember about you? How will you make the best impression? It's better to not talk too much, stay focused on the points you want to make and answer questions directly and to the point.

If you get through this phone interview, you will likely be scheduled to meet in person. The in person meeting can be the final interview, or can be one of the final steps. Several other meetings may be scheduled, primarily a meeting with the hiring manager's boss, hiring manager's peers, or other team members that would be working with you. All of their impressions will go into the final decision. Some companies even have you do a presentation in front of all of these people, all at once. They might ask you to talk about your background and interests, or they could ask you to present on a product you know and talk about why they would want to buy it (common for sales roles). They may try to intimidate you or lob objections at you to see how you handle it. I've heard of all of these things happening, so it's best to be prepared and let no situation be a surprise, just roll with it and keep a sense of humor.

In-Person Interview

This interview is important because the interview represents a few different things to the person who is interviewing you. First, it's a confirmation that you really are as you "appear" on paper. Meaning, your resume represented a person who had solid skills, experience and fit the job description. Can you articulate the same "professionalism, knowledge, experience" in person as you appear on paper or over the phone? If they ask you to tell them about your experience, they don't need you to read the resume, they want to hear how you respond, with confidence, representing the same "success" and skills they expected or not. It's an impression issue more than it is one of facts and figures.

Second, it's a chance to see if you represent yourself professionally, meaning, you look like you fit into the company, you dress appropriately, communicate well, you have good manners, make eye contact and appear confident. Also, that your appearance leaves a positive impression. This means neatness counts, the style of your clothing, appropriate dress to the company style and look and how you look overall. The elements of an appearance should consider all of the following things.

- Style is current but conservative. This means you are wearing a current hairstyle, current clothing, and stylish fitted business clothing, but the colors are neutral to plain.
- Jewelry is tasteful and simple, shoes match but are not too high or open-toed, and so on. Nothing loud rather, conservative on each of these areas.
- If you are older and are wearing bouffant hair-do or a Farrah Fawcett haircut, you likely look out of style.
- if you have on slouchy pants, open shoes, or have piercings/tattoos, though this might be a current style, it is not conservative.

You might look through some ads for clothing at places where people shop for business clothes such as major department stores or specialty stores and look through their catalogs and try to assemble something similar.

One way to assess whether you look "right" for the interview is to identify the dress code for that company or industry and dress up one or two levels. You can observe people leaving that office to see what they wear a few days prior to the interview, or you can ask people you know what type of dress code this company or industry has.

Even if the company is business casual it's important to dress up a level or two for an interview, meaning if they don't wear ties and suits, they are business casual, then you should wear a suit with no tie, or dress pants and a jacket with no tie and nice shoes such as those worn with a suit. For women, a dress with a jacket is always appropriate or a suit (pants or skirt) with a nice blouse works. Teetering heels and open toed shoes, tight tops or plunging necklines are out. Loose and fitted for either sex is best. If you do happen to be meeting where the dress code is "startup" such as flip-flops and shorts, you should wear nice pants and a nice golf shirt, again, dressing up is key. You want them to think, "he looks nice" or "he/she is dressing stylish for today" but from there, focus on you.

Third, the person interviewing you wants to make sure you really can really PERFORM the job AND you WANT the job or at least, are interested and want to proceed through the interview process. So you need to show up with the job description, a copy of the resume you did for this job application printed on nice upgraded paper, and some research on the company (what the company does, who their clients are, their current stock market valuation, recent news, how is the company doing financially, any strategies around acquisitions/ downsizing recently?) This information can be found on their website and also in their annual report and recent news). If you know anyone who has interviewed at this firm or was hired recently, this person might share what questions were asked and what type of people are currently being hired.

You should have crafted a list of questions from your research to specifically assess if the company is a fit for you and how you think you will fit the culture and job challenges. These questions will not only ask for information but represent that you know something about the company , the job, the industry, and their expectations. Though you may be willing to take any job, appearing selective and thoughtful makes you more attractive as a candidate. An attitude of eagerness can appear desperate, i.e., I'll take any job I can get. You need to appear selective, and you can appear selective by having done this research on the job, the culture, and the expectations of the company about dress-code, appearance and job responsibilities. The questions you ask reflect your level of knowledge AND your level of interest, so craft them carefully.

An example would be "I read that the company has acquired 4 or 5 smaller firms recently, and I've always been interested in mergers and acquisitions, I considered this major in college. Can you share with me the company's acquisition strategy?". This question communicates that you did research on the company, are interested in mergers and acquisitions (which is good if this is their strategy for growth) and want to understand more about this strategy. I believe that you need to be prepared to answer questions from any statement you make, so be careful to not lie or make false statements. I can imagine the interviewer asking you " what type of classes in mergers and acquisitions did you take in college?, i.e., Why were you interested in this area?"

Another important thing to communicate is what YOU are looking for. People who know what they want typically get what they want. If you don't have a clear idea of what you are looking for in a company, job, career, or life in general, you might appear like an open book with no direction or a close-minded person with a narrow view. Being able to highlight 3-5 things that are must haves for you in a job/company shows that you know what you want. Make sure these things are realistic, and humble, (Stating, "I want to be president of the company by the time I'm 26 years old" isn't a realistic statement. Rather, say, "I'd like to move into management and am looking for a company where I can take on new responsibilities, though I recognize that I have to achieve in each role to earn that privilege".

Saying that you are ready for a change, or you need to get a job isn't the right message. Rather saying you are looking to do _____type of work (_____fits the job description). Also, if you know that the job requires travel, long hours, or meeting with clients, you might mention you like to travel and work face to face with clients and want to find a job that allows you to do this. The more you know about the job, the company culture and their expectations, the more you can customize your list of 3-5 Job desires for this position.

Finally the person who is interviewing you wants to know if you are going to fit in. If the culture is very buttoned-up and rules oriented, they will want to assess if you are someone who is a free spirit or functions well in an organization with structure. That is why the research into the company matters so much, you should avoid cultures where you don't feel you will be happy or fit in. This requires you know yourself well enough to know what you don't want, then make sure you try to understand as much as possible about the culture of this company before you interview. If you don't have this information, be making that assessment while interviewing. You can tell by how people dress and act whether the environment is more formal or more informal. If the company has a lot of employee turnover, that could be a good sign or a bad sign. It's bad if they are too demanding, unrealistic, or workaholic, high pressure environment. This is good if people who work here are being picked off by other companies because their experience and skill is in high demand. Once you get through the interview, and they express interest in you, you can ask to talk to one or two other people in your role. You can ask them why they chose that company and what the culture is like.

Executive Meetings

An Executive is someone who has a higher level of responsibility and normally a title to go with it. A "C" level executive might be a Sr. VP, VP, Chief _____(Information Officer, Accounting Officer, Financial Officer, etc.). Typically meeting with an executive and/or talking to them on the phone requires a certain type of finesse that might be different than the in-person discussion with a hiring manager. An executive has little time and typically a shorter attention span. These people often fall into a "Driver" type personality. Normally, these people are highly busy, go from meeting to meeting, and make decisions based on information at hand, often within a short timeframe. Therefore, this person might view their role in the interview process to make a quick assessment on skills and fit, then give the hiring manager their blessing. It's best to know something about the executive before any interview or meeting. This is where your 3-5 key points about why you should be hired or why you fit for this job is important. You want to present a positive interest, and leave him/her with the impression you know what you want and it happens to be a fit with what they are looking for. This will make it easy for the executive to give you the nod.

Discussing Pay and Compensation Plans

For many people, pay and benefits along with work environment, the opportunity to learn new things and the ability to advance are key to the decision on whether or not to accept a position. They are also key factors in keeping a person from leaving a position. If people do not feel adequately recognized, rewarded and given opportunities to expand and grow to other roles in the company, they can become frustrated. So too often, while interviewing, we want to ask about these things early on, to make sure that there is a fit with what we are expecting. However, its difficult and can be uncomfortable to bring up compensation, work-life balance, recognition, benefits or other areas because they are best brought up by the hiring manager at the right time; the right time is when you have passed the initial recruiter and hiring manager discussion, and they are asking you, well are you interested? In so many words, they will be testing the water to see if you are interested in going to the next step. How can you be interested without knowing the answers to these questions?

There are a number of ways to find out more about the answers to these questions without coming right out and asking what the job pays, what the working hours are, if you can work from home sometimes, if you will get a chance to be recognized (a club trip or other awards) and what type of other benefits the company can offer you. The below are a number of ways you can ask some questions early on, specifically, *when talking to the recruiter* preferably or with the hiring manager only after she asks if you want move forward to the next step. You can now research how the opportunity fits with your goals. Some things you should ask:
What are the components of the compensation and reward plan at this company? I.e. how are people incented and awarded for outstanding performance at this company? *What this means*: Is there a salary, a bonus structure, a profit sharing plan, and stock options?
This question can also lead the recruiter to ask what you are looking for in a compensation plan, does this plan type meet your expectations? What type of salary are you looking for or expecting? This is a loaded question. The best way to answer is with a range. Having done your homework, you can say for example $35k-65k for the compensation package. The "package" is broad enough to imply it's not all salary in the package. If you are able to get to this point in the conversation, likely they will say the salary is more in the _____range so you at least now know more of what they will pay. *Never say it doesn't matter, I'm flexible. This implies they can low- ball your pay, and they will, and when you find out after the fact that you are not paid what others get, you will not be happy. Then it will be too late to fix it.*

1. How are people awarded for their performance at this company?

2. What is the career path for this position? What other opportunities are there beyond this position? How long does it typically take for someone to advance in this company? This may lead to a discussion about how ambitious you are. This can be a good or bad thing. If your ambition is to be President before you are 30, it's likely not viewed that you will be happy in this entry position. That's not good. On the other hand, if you want to be able to try different roles and learn different aspects of the business, this is more indicative of someone who is promotable.

3. What are some of the things that make employees want to work for this company? Is there much turnover? Do people stay here for many years? If so, what about the company makes people want to stay here longer term?

The recruiter may not know this. The hiring manager will. If they highlight soft benefits like a casual Friday or flexible work schedule, they might not pay as well as some other firms. However, if they talk about financial rewards and that is important to you, then in fact they will likely allow you to make more money here. You could say something like the below:

"I've heard that _____ is a family friendly company, (if you have heard that) what about the company makes it great for someone with a family to work here?" If they can't answer this question, likely they don't think that is a focus of the company. If it is a focus, they will bring up things like flexible schedules, great family benefits, better vacations, reward trips, etc. If you have heard that the company is not family friendly, try to ask why people stay here longer term? What about the company incents people to stay?

4. Can you give me some examples of advancement opportunities at this company where people who took this position ended up 3-5 years later? You don't want to hear that most are in the same job This will tell you what the path to get more money and responsibility looks like at this company

Benefits are an area that many people who are over 40 years old took for granted for many years. In the 1980s to early 1990's companies paid 100% of family benefits for medical, dental, vision, and retirement funds (Pensions or 401k matches). There were no deductions or copayments. Now many companies require employees to contribute to these plans, and these contributions can be steep in cost. Typically for medical, dental and vision plans, along with drug/prescription benefits, the out of pocket can be $200-700/month for a family, and then there are the deductibles that have to be paid by you before the insurance kicks in. Finally, some of the plans are capped (not to exceed in a given year or lifetime) and may not include some types of procedures that you might need. So finding out about the benefits DOES matter. A company who pays for almost a full set of benefits with minimum out of pocket means more money in your pocket. People do not usually talk at all about benefits until they are being offered the job. They often find out about the benefits after they accept the job and have access to the benefit system. One way to find out about the generosity of the benefits is to request to talk to some recent hires (1 year or less onboard) about the position, and what it entails. These people are not interviewing you. They are people who already work there, you are going to be offered a job, and you want to talk to someone who is working there about the job. So you can ask the hiring manager if you can talk to some teammates or peers. You can ask some of these people valuable questions that only someone who is not following a script can answer honestly. Interesting things to glean from these people include:

- Do most people here make their goals/bonus objectives or just a small percent?
- Is there a lot of employee turnover?
- Do you see a lot of opportunity long term here for your career, why or why not?
- How would you compare the benefits package with others you have seen, does it cover most everything or is it a lot of out of pocket cost?

I have learned a lot from these types of discussions. If I know the person or am acquainted with them, I've even asked them if the range of pay x to y is a fair amount to expect or more or less then they think most people are paid. I've had people tell me what salary they were offered right off the bat and they might tell you what some recent hires got as well.

On a final note, I will tell you that during a long career with many companies, I have been lied to about a number of things during an interview. I've had hiring managers avoid answering my questions about compensation, and give me a range of what people can make in the job as far as the real total earnings. In several of these cases, they knew what I was making and what monies I was leaving on the table when I departed my old role. I have two stories to tell here, and a lesson can be learned from both. If someone can't share with you the exact salary, target income, objectives/goals/quotas, and compensation components when offering you the job, they are likely not being truthful with you.

I've had people low-ball offers to me and then later, I found that others got higher offers, no questions asked. How did they do it? What did these other people do differently? They did not have to negotiate anything Many of these people were men, which is telling, but not all men are treated this way. The people who had the offers that were correct were perceived as being difficult to entice to join the business, harder to get so to speak, or knew the hiring manager personally, so the offers were straight- out better and higher end then what I was offered. It's often written that women are underpaid by 30% of what a man is paid. Lots of studies have been done and many come to the conclusion women can't negotiate, take breaks for babies, need more flexible schedules, work in lower paying industries or positions, or don't like to talk about money because it's not considered polite. I don't believe this is the case for all of these situations. I believe that there is a "sticky floor" out there. There is a perception that women will accept less so are offered less. Since the hiring manager doesn't pay the salary, there is no reason for them to NOT offer you what you are worth. This makes it all the more important to know what people are getting offered for what years/type of experience so you can make a clear statement early on what you expect to be paid.

Due to the poor economy, now many recent graduates, both men and women, find themselves in the same situation. Unfortunately, if you are a woman, you may have to deal with this situation more often than a man. If you are a man who was underpaid or had a bad situation at a job and couldn't make a full amount of bonus due to things outside of your control, you could get a low-ball offer. You might find people asking what you made at your last job to try to make that the baseline for this new one. So It's key to go to the table with an idea of what you *should be paid* and be prepared to respond to push back on what packages they can get you based on your past job's pay. On the other hand, having an outsized demand doesn't work either, expecting to get much more than your worth in the market is not possible.

The research and homework you do up front is key. In some companies, there is little salary movement over long periods of time. Rather, people get ahead via commissions, bonuses, and other forms of rewards. Titles can even change, but *salary where you started is the baseline for any raises awarded* and if it's too low, you may never get ahead. Its often said, "you have to leave this company and come back to get more money here." This is a common theme in many companies. They reward those who change often over those who stay and perform. So it's best to start at a level you feel is competitive. Underpayment makes for bad feelings about your job.

Below are some compensation stories that are true stories. This will help you to see how these types of discussions evolve and the vagueness you often encounter in these discussions can work against you:

Compensation story #1. *At the time when I got this job offer, I was 28 years old and was working for four years at a company that was my first business job out of college. The company where I worked, call is "DataXYZ" had many fits and stops, laying off people and there was some question on whether or not the company was going to survive longer term. This was a sales position.*

They had two different compensation plans, one for recent college graduates range of pay was about $25,000-$29,000, and senior salespeople in their 30s or 40s and these people got a range of pay that was $36,000-$39,000 depending on what they negotiated. This was pretty straight forward and the commission structure was X % up to 100% of your quota and Y% over your quota. Very simple. These types of plans were very common for sales roles.

In contrast, another company "ABC" was a leader in its industry, a very difficult place to even get an interview, never mind a job, and many people working there had stayed there for their entire career. There was very little information about what this company paid, because most of their employees were hired right out of college and were top 5% of graduating class. They had just started a professional hire program, where they sought out people who were currently at competitors. They wanted to put these people into their key accounts where competitors were strongest, and use their already developed sales acumen to stop the competition.

I was out one evening at a restaurant and walked to the bar for a drink while waiting for a friend. The man sitting there started chatting with me. He indicated he worked at ABC and I laughed and said "Oh, weird, I work at DataXYZ". He started saying that ABC had an edge over DataXYZ but for some reason, in certain types of accounts (Engineering/Manufacturing), DataXYZ was killing them. I told him why I thought that was. He was very interested and pushed back on a few points. I pushed right back at him. We did hit it off. He was a very down-to-earth person and was genuinely interested in what I had to say. He asked me if I would ever consider working for ABC. I said possibly, it so happened I was currently interviewing with another company TX that competed with both DataXYZ and ABC but it was primarily because they were pursuing me for a specific role in the same accounts as I had at DataXYZ. I pointed out my interest level was low because I felt it was unethical to go back into the same accounts with another company and the same product. He offered me his card. His card said VP Sales ABC Company. I gave him my card as well. He said "I'm going to call you."

The following week on Monday, I got a call from him personally asking me to schedule a time to come in. I accepted and went to see him. He introduced me to about 5 other people there. What I thought was an hour interview ended up being about 4 hours of meeting people. The other people were managers in the same branch who worked for him. He was high up there. I was pretty flattered.

At the end of long day, he asked me if I wanted the job. I frankly told him, I don't know enough about it, for example, what is the pay structure? I have a lot of business on the table, I told him, and many years of investment in my current patch. He indicated that people there make over 100 % of their target incomes every year. He wanted to know what my current salary was. I told him, but I also told him that I had money on the table ($25-30k at least) of business that was closing, along with a full pipeline of opportunity. Additionally, I was being considered for a promotion to a Sr. Sales Person at the end of that year. That would entail the $36k base salary and a target income that was higher at quota. He left the room and came back, his words to me were "I can offer you a

$48k salary "and at quota you would make about $95-100k. In my current role at DataXYZ, I could make that if the sales I was working came in. But that salary was big to me. I had just gotten married, bought a bigger house, and needed as much cash flow as I could get. I said to put it in writing and Id consider it.

The next week, I got two offer letters, one from ABC and one from TX; $52,000 for TX and $48,000 for ABC. TX had said they would pay out only about $38,000 of that as salary and the remainder was the value of the benefits including profit sharing and car benefits. The TX role offered a company car, easily worth $8k / year to me. This company car included the car, all the insurance, gas / car washes / maintenance. However, as mentioned before, the opportunity at TX was to go into the same accounts with a competitive product. The salary wasn't much better than my promoted role at DataXYZ. This wasn't too appealing to me. I had offers in hand, what to do? The thought process back then (1980s) was that if you pick a company to work for, you might stay there your entire career. Today, you wouldn't probably think that way. Today, I would have gone back to my manager at DataXYZ to see if a competitive offer was warranted. Then I would have considered all options, talked to some people, found out more what the culture was like. But frankly, being recruited by a top company (both TX and ABC) and offered a nice uplift in salary at 28 years old was very flattering. So I accepted ABCs offer.

I started at ABC and one thing I noticed up front was that while DataXYZ was a very entrepreneurial company. There you worked on your own and anything you wanted to put together to win a deal was considered. At ABC it was much more structured. People interacted a lot and business was less urgent, much more long-term focused. You had to get everyone to agree first, before you took any action. I found this culture somewhat stifling. Additionally, for the first three months, I was considered to be salary only, no quota or commission options because I was learning the ropes. At the end of the 3 months, my manager called me in his office to talk about the quota. He offered me the quota and indicated what the payout would be. He showed me a one page document and it said something like this "Salary Equivalent $21,600, Salary target $48,000, and quota target $82,000". This isn't exact but this is the memory I have. It turns out they had a 40-60 type pay plan, and the way they worded it, the salary was not the salary, in fact, it was a number in the middle of a range. The "salary equivalent" was the take home pay! The offer letter had stated that my salary was $48k! There was no document stating this pay plan was the actual pay. Here I would end up with $15k less than at DataXYZ and $2,400 less than my existing salary. Additionally, the take home was less than what I would have gotten at TX. I was devastated.

I was stuck. Everyone there was on that type of plan and went about thinking it was ok. Most joined out of college, so it was all they knew. I didn't know what to do. ABC had a suggestion box that was anonymous. I put a note in there stating what had happened. I felt I had been lied to and misled deliberately about the pay. It turns out, that several other people had also the same experience, specifically professional hires from other companies or other roles at ABC who had moved into this team. *The VP got in trouble and ended up leaving the company. I felt very bad about this, because I liked him personally.*

Afterwards, I was told, "We can raise your 'salary equivalent' a few thousand dollars by raising your salary target. The managed to do something that brought me to $123k, less than my prior job but close to the amount I was making at the time I left in salary. I found out two years later that another professional hire from another company had received a much higher salary and was on a special compensation plan because the plans that ABC had were too low for him to leave his prior employer. Apparently, he got special treatment and I did not. I decided to leave and after 4 years, I departed for another firm who never treated me with anything but honesty and respect. Incidentally, since that time, I have never run into this type of verbiage or situation with offer letters that mislead the person on the salary.

Compensation Story #2. *I was much older and wiser when this happened to me, but what I found from this experience is that sometimes, the hiring manager is careless about throwing numbers around that aren't accurate and its difficult to find someone at the company to tell you what the numbers really are. Some might say false information is deliberate, but in fact, companies change managers and compensation plans for some jobs every few years and the manager might be new or not know about upcoming changes.*
The job I interviewed for was a role that paid a higher salary and a lower target income then other roles at this company. Figuring out if the salary and target income were right for me was the challenge. The organization I was joining had gone through some massive changes and the manager was new to his role and had moved over from another role and retained his same salary and a higher target income, so he might not have known or bothered to research what people should be paid coming from the outside. He offered me a salary and indicated the target

income at the quota was about $100k higher than the salary, but really, people make 20k-30k more than that in a typical year. I checked in with a few people I knew at this company, hey , does this sound right to you. One person in particular had been in this same role 4 years earlier and said yes, that is in line with what he had seen. I asked them for a signing bonus, indicating I was leaving money on the table. The hiring manager said they didn't offer signing bonuses but that the quota was divided in 4 equal quarterly amounts and I would receive payment of $25k or 100% for the first quarter and the payment was not a recoverable draw, rather it was non-recoverable. This is how they handle the first quarter every year he told me. I asked it be put in the offer letter, and he said that since it's a commission payment, it wouldn't be listed.

After I joined the company, the $25k never arrived during my first three months on the job. The person who was supposed to be my manager, the guy who hired me, moved to another role the first week I was on the job. My new manager was told about the $25k commitment and he scrambled around to try and get to the bottom of it. He commented to me that in the past (two years prior, not recent) they used to have a program like this one but it no longer was in existence. He offered me a

$20k recoverable draw, meaning I had to pay it back with other monies I made later in the year. In the meantime, I had not received any type of compensation plan and it was month 5 on the job! The compensation plan would have defined the target quota, commissions, bonuses and targets for measurement on the job. Finally towards the middle of month 5, I received the plan. The target income showed $30k less than what I'd been told. When I asked my new boss about why the target income was so low, I did not say anything about the misleading target income discussions I had with the former manager. I had already complained about the $25k so didn't want to appear like a complete idiot. His comment was the quota was low due to the new nature of my role and the territory having not been covered so that was likely the reason. Needless to say, I now found out that had I expected that target income, I would have been offered a salary that was $20k higher. Now here I am underpaid for the skills I brought in. I received raises over the years and my performance was excellent. But no matter the raises, typically 2-3% a year at most, I could hardly climb out of so deep a hole.

The last leg of this story is the worst I think. There was a year when the economy was very bad. I was having a record year, but my organization was doing very poorly. One executive decided we needed a drastic change to our compensation plans. He announced that we were going to move from a plan that was 65% salary and 35% commission/bonus to one that was 50/50; this In the next two weeks. The next day I received a letter in the mail stating though my target income (still too low) was the same, my salary was to become half of that, so would drop by $32k. The letter also stated that my employment was at the company discretion, (i.e. don't think about hiring an attorney or objecting). While pay plans can change, so drastic a change done so thoughtlessly was really shocking. The solution should have been so simple; Management should have been able to identify those who were top performers and make an adjustment to their salary so the change was much less drastic, bringing their target income up to a higher level so the change could be justified as a benefit; i.e. you'll make more money in a typical year.

They did none of this. Many people left because they were being underpaid. They hired a lot of new people, and guess what? Many of these new people got target incomes that were lower than my initial salary but as much as $15k higher than my current salary. Their target incomes were therefore, 30k higher than my current lower salary after the cut. Why would they do that? Well, they couldn't find and hire people for these types of salaries and target incomes, so they made an upward adjustment for new people. Also, having a manager who wasn't willing to fight to make sure I got better treatment meant that some of my peers were able to recover half their lost salary while I only recovered 20% of mine through raises over time.

The moral of these two stories is many. Did I scare you? I hope so. People do not realize that this type of thing goes on all the time. Many people just don't talk about it, they put it behind them and either find a different job or accept it. The main lesson to learn here is, get the pay right up-front, otherwise, you will pay the price personally for being underpaid for years to come. You will find out you are underpaid and it causes resentment and that resentment seethes under the surface and affects your happiness, well-being and can even negatively affect your job performance.

If you know any recruiters or if you don't, use LinkedIn to track a few independent recruiters down, and find out what the pay ought to be. Ask to talk to some people who have been in the job a while and ask some of the leading questions listed above, what type of target incomes do people really make here? Do bonuses get paid out at 100% typically? Are there many chances for raises and promotions? You can ask this and not be invading the privacy of the person. If you have some rapport with them, you might even say I'm being offered 110-130k (say you were offered 112k) and ask if that is the average pay, high end or low end of the pay scale?

Finally, if you end up working for someone who isn't your advocate, you need to work harder to find other advocates in the company who will speak for you so you can get your raises and recognition. The expression, *'the writing is on the wall'* applies here. If the manager you work for is weak and not politically connected or inclined, or doesn't like you for any reason, get away from them and move to another position in the company, otherwise, you will have to accept your situation. You also will fall further behind your peers in pay and promotion. Having mentors and advocates who will look out for you is key in any job.

A final note on this topic is about overpayment. If you find that you were offered more than most people get for your position and experience, you might find that when it's time to cut cost or eliminate people, the high cost person will go. Or you may have excellent performance, but since your pay is outsized, you are passed over for raises until it matches or is under your peers or other new people hired. Its best to get what is typically offered on average or possibly in a best case, the lower end of the top 25% quartile.

Questions They Might Ask You During an Interview

Below are some of the questions you might be asked during an interview and recommendations for preparing the answers in advance. Know what you are going to say when a type of question is asked. What they want to find out is the following: Can you do the job? Do you want the job and are willing to work to keep it? Will you really like this work? Can we tolerate having you work here, meaning, will you fit in and get along with people? Are you a problem solver, here to make the company a success or are you a problem causer, all about your own needs and wants? Answer these questions in advance:

- What can you tell me about yourself?
- Looking at your resume, tell me about XYZ job, what did you do there, why did you leave?
- Looking at your resume, it says here you developed 75 new clients, tell me more about these clients and how you found them and developed them.
- What did you learn at XYZ job?
- What is your biggest strength? Your biggest weakness? What was your biggest success? Your biggest failure? What did you learn from it?
- Where do you want to be in 5 years? What are your career goals?
- Why are you interested in working for XYZ? What about our company caught your eye?
- What type of work do you really want to do?
- How would you handle a certain situation (difficult colleague who participates negatively or not at all in a team assignment, a difficult client, pressure for a deadline)? He might ask to give some examples of other times you have had to deal with these things.
- How would you handle a specific job challenge pertinent to this job. Example if it's a finance job, perhaps they give an example of financial reports that indicate sales are going down rather than up. What type of things would you do to get to the bottom of the reasons why? If you are a teacher, they could pose a question about a student who starts the year strong but seems to be falling off a cliff academically and emotionally, and failing by midyear, how would you help that student?
- What can you offer this company that makes you different from others?
- Do you have a mentor and if so, who is the mentor and why?
- What would your current colleagues say about you? Your direct reports? You Managers?
- What are your hobbies?

- What is the last book you read (business and personal fun book) and what about it did you enjoy the most?
- Who is our CEO? Who are our competitors? What is the leading product we sell? What are our focus areas for the upcoming year?
- Do you think of yourself as lucky? Why or why not?

Questions They Won't Ask and Things You Should Not Say or Do During an Interview

They may ask about personal things but without any direct intent to pry into areas that ought to not be considered during a job interview. Sometimes the interviewer can inadvertently share that they are married, have children or participate heavily in outside activities that take up personal time. Some people may feel this is an opening to share the same. I believe you should not share too many personal details for a number of reasons, but primarily, though, people have unknown prejudices and pre-conceived notions that are best left out of the job discussion. They might ask if you have any issues with travel. You should say no. However, if you really DO have an issue with travel, later in the meeting you might ask them what type of travel requirements the job has. This way, you are getting the information you need at a different time in the conversation. It's not legal for them to ask whether you have children, have a nanny or childcare, can travel or not due to having children or plans to have children. They can't ask about your age, race or marital status, or any healthcare issues. You should NOT share any of these things either. People have ideas about other people and their situations that may not be accurate. I once worked for a man who gave me less responsibility then others, and when I complained, he looked surprised that I wanted to travel. After all, I had kids at home and husband who worked, didn't I? He didn't intend to reveal that he had a pre-conceived notion about this situation that was clearly inaccurate.

They should not and typically will not act inappropriately towards you such as make comments about your dress/clothing, your appearance or any other personal items unless it's something nonchalant or impersonal compliment.

You should not say or do any of the following things – the DON'TS:

- Arrive late for the interview
- Talk loudly or play loud games or texts while waiting for your interview on your cell phone.
- Turn off the phone or put it on silent before entering the lobby of the building. Read a company magazine in the lobby. Put the phone away.
- Not know the name of the person you are meeting with or sifting through your bag for the name of the person. Know the spelling as well and if the receptionist can't find the person, indicate you have their contact information and cell phone should she/he need it to locate them.

- Fail to address anyone you meet including the receptionist by name and fail to be just as friendly and courteous to all people at the company as you are to the interviewer.
- Failure to make eye contact with everyone you speak to at the company.
- Failing to shake hands firmly with anyone who is being introduced to you. State, "hello my name is _____, shake hands, "it's nice to meet you".
- Failing to bring a copy of your resume printed on fine paper along with several reference letters.
- Asking questions or making statements that make you appear negative or clueless such as
  - What sort of perks do you offer?
  - My boss is a real jerk or I really hated that company.
  - What does your company do?
  - "I love your" suit, glasses, tie, shoes or pictures of his family.
  - Complaining about your health in any way or making any inference to having been sick.
  - Stating you were fired from any position. If you were let go and they specifically ask why you left, either you left for a different opportunity or you could state that position you had was eliminated.
  - Make it appear that you just want any job and are desperate. Its best to be there for the job you applied for and for specific types of jobs, not for any job.
  - Saying I don't know to a question and therefore, missing the opportunity to show some knowledge and confidence. If you are asked a question about yourself personally, you should know the answer. If it's a question about something factual such as your exact GPA when graduating from high school, you can say "I think it was a 3.4 but I can find out and get back to you on the exact number by end of day if you would like". If it's a hypothetical question (something strange such as how many M&Ms can fit in this jar? or how would I write code to solve the following problem....") for these types of questions, they just want to see how you would think the problem through. You should describe what you might do to go about estimating the answer (Such as volume of the jar and approx volume of the M&M, etc).
  - Making statements about your strengths, I work hard, or your weaknesses, I have trouble getting up in the morning. These are too vague and don't leave a positive impression. Your strength

should be a strength that would benefit this company for this job and your weakness should be something that isn't a personality flaw and can even be seen as a benefit. For example, my strength is my persistence, I don't give up easily and whenever a door closes, I believe a window opens. My weakness is that I'm not the most patient person, I like to see action happen and to make it happen.

I believe that it's ok to learn something about the person you are interviewing with before arriving at the interview. You can do a Google search and find the person online and see if they published any articles or participated in any events. You can find them on Linked-in and read about their background. It's a good idea to be friendly enough to glean some items about the interviewer, because it allows for a more personal commonality between both parties. For example, if there is a picture on the desk showing the interviewer with their kids wearing a baseball uniform, you can always ask how old their children are and tell them your son played baseball too. This approach opens up a more friendly line of communication without overstepping professional boundaries.

What to Wear and Body Language

What to wear to an interview was discussed earlier but bears repeating. You should dress UP one notch from the company standard. If the standard is a golf shirt and nice pants with casual but dressy shoes, you should wear a suit with a jacket or sports jacket and a nice shirt, no tie. If the dress code is jeans and tennis shoes, you might wear nice pants and a suit shirt with no tie. The idea being, you want to stand out and look "nice" while not looking clueless to their dress code or out of place. Should you overdress, you can always remove your jacket which automatically dresses you down a level. If you are a woman, overdressing is somewhat more difficult. A dress is always nice but if its paired with a jacket, the jacket can be removed to reflect a more casual look. A pants suit always looks nice and a skirt and jacket suit is perfectly appropriate for both casual and business casual. I would not recommend jeans, open toed shoes, or overly casual dress to be on the safe side for the first interview and never for an interview with an executive.

Body language communicates more about you than you think, so you should be conscious of your facial expressions, hand gestures, posture, and overall body positioning. Voice tone and quality of speech tells a lot about someone. You want to appear self-assured, not cocky, and confident but interested in learning more. There are certain ways of sitting and talking that can make people believe what you are saying or wonder if you are lying. There are books and articles about this topic and they are worth reading to understand the impression you might be sending. A few that can be highlighted include:

- Sitting back in a chair with your arms crossed in front of you may mean you are not open to ideas or discussion—sit forward in your chair slightly, feet on the floor, and steeple your fingers together or use your hands for small gestures to make a point (no waving of hands wildly).
- Not making eye contact or a wimpy handshake makes you seem nervous and lacking confidence. Look at the person directly. Try to smile occasionally or add some levity to make the meeting less uncomfortable. Take notes, that will allow you to look down on occasion or reference the notes you brought with you and breaks the uncomfortable feeling of staring at someone too long.
- Talking too fast, and too monotone, shows nervousness and distracts from what you are saying. If you documented and reviewed the answers to the questions that will be asked of you in the interview, you should be able to answer succinctly and clearly with confidence. Try to speak in a way that is a story telling style, at a normal pace, not too slowly, rather than a rehearsed speech. "well, I'm glad you asked me that question. I was thinking about this the other day and

_____" or "That is an interesting question. There are probably a few things, but I think the number one thing is _____".

- Touching your face (left ear, nose) shows you might be lying specifically with your left hand.
- Swirling your hair or twitching, including shaking your foot, makes you appear less confident and nervous.

If the interviewer is doing any of these things, it may be telling about the way the interview is going or something about how the interviewer and their own style:

- Sitting back in their seat, with feet on the desk, arms crossed or behind their head, these can be signs of power, i.e. I am the powerful one, the person in charge. The only reason this matters is it tells you that the person is likely someone who values their power and their position and wants you to respect it.
- The person looks at their watch a lot. They may want to appear busy or in a hurry. So that person is telling you inadvertently their time is limited so don't waste it. No idle chit-chat, get to the point.
- The person wants to chit-chat on idle topics. This is just a style issue. Some people want to make you feel comfortable. Just respond but keep the answers shorter and to the point. The one thing that can go wrong with chit-chatting too much is you might create too casual of a relationship for a solid interview outcome but worse, time can run out and the interview isn't completed. Another candidate might be able to complete the interview and that could work against you.
- The person asks a lot of rote questions and shows no interest or enthusiasm on the answers you provide. It's possible a decision was made already and they are just completing the interview with you because it was scheduled.

Personal Branding

Personal branding is both a formal and an informal thing. Some people actually hire a "brand" manager or a career coach to help them sell their brand. The idea behind this is there are an image and a set of expertise to advertise, and one needs to figure out the best way to communicate that message. Where branding can include your resume, your Linked-in and online profile, your role as a leader in the organization or industry you are in, along with other formal criterion, branding can also be as simple as the fact that "perception is reality". If people perceive you a certain way, they believe you are that way, whether or not this true. This is a first impression issue, and since finding a job involves a lot of first impressions, I felt that covering some branding discussion might cause you to think more about what impression you make.

Branding is really public relations. Celebrities have a PR person who will create an image for them and then help them market this image. Branding is managing people's impressions of you. How people experience you and how others feel about you at the end of that interaction makes a big difference in your ability to win a job and a sponsor. It's also critical to long term career success. You really have to ask yourself, how do I WANT to be perceived by others. What do I want them to think about me, feel about me? If you start here by making a list under three topic:

How do I want to be perceived during an initial meeting(list up to five words)
How do I want people to _feel a_bout me after interacting with me (list up to five words)
What do I want them to think about me after the interaction is over? (list up to five words)

Think about some famous people such as Oprah Winfrey, Katie Couric, or Barbara Walters. These people each have a very strong brand. People are impressed with them and are left thinking and feeling they were HEARD, UNDERSTOOD, CARED ABOUT, and HELPED by the interaction. They didn't feel "judged" or as if they made a mistake by sharing personal information. The interaction was freeing, left them feeling as if they were on the road to healing, and had a new friend and ally. These people set out to create a brand that produced these results, it's no accident. Others who have a brand that is different are world leaders. Leaders have a persona, some leaders have a negative power, they are threatening, powerful, somewhat frightening, such as Adolf Hitler. Others have a positive power like Ronald Reagan, on the surface they are smiling, pleasant and nonchalant. Again, this is a deliberate set of behaviors to leave others feeling a certain way about them. People may forget what you said or did but not how you made them feel.

These people associated themselves with others who create a similar brand, the same type of positive or negative outcome or feelings. So you will see Oprah with Dr. Phil, Dr. Oz, Dr. Laura, or Nate Berkus. All of these people have a similar brand to Oprah. So these relationships enhance her brand. The importance of this is that one can associate with a lot of different people in a career, but those who climb the ladder are surrounded by others with a similar brand.

They do this on purpose, because they realize that it's not just what they do and say, how they say it, but who they say it to that makes a difference in their brand.

Successful branding is both a plan and a process for building that plan into a reality. Some people have natural abilities that lead to a certain type of brand. Its best to know yourself and aspire to new heights, rather than try to be someone you are not.

The number one quality (if you are lucky enough to have it) that inspires a personal brand is charisma or personal charm. Some people have a quality that inspires devotion so that makes being a leader easier for these people. Even if you aren't born with natural charm, you can create charisma by doing some of the following things.

- Positive attitude.
- Focus 100% in on people in the moment, don't let your mind wander when others are speaking.
- A strong communicator, make ideas simple and to the point, don't ramble or over talk.
- Be authentic, not fake. Do you believe what you are saying with all your heart?
- Be empathetic and likeable. Exude warmth and caring.
- Focus on a bigger goal, the larger organization, rather than what you can gain personally from any interaction.
- Your brand involves a few things that say something about you. Tell stories or talk about things that emphasize your beliefs and actions around your brand. Example, Oprah's Angel Network story or stories of how Oprah helped girls in Africa with a boarding school.

Finally, not everyone is going to be a CEO or wants to be in charge. But all people should exude a persona or personal power that causes others to take notice of you and respect and appreciate your contributions. This can include:

- Showing some vulnerability which makes you approachable.
- Knowledge about specific topics, where others seek you out because of expertise.
- Strong communications to get to a point quickly.

- Resilience, embraces change.
- Leadership in demonstrating emotional intelligence. Reading people's emotions and listening to what they are really trying to say, not just focusing on what is being said.
- Your personal power will increase if you have influence that goes below you to others who are your subordinate, your peers and your company's leaders.
- Try to communicate with people the way they want to communicate, in person, text, phone or email, if someone is inclined to pick up the phone and call you rather than email, then you call them rather than sending them email.

Follow-up After the Interview

Before going to an interview, it's important to highlight soft skills required today to land a new job. Soft skills are a combination of knowing how to present yourself to an employer (the process and appropriate presentation of any materials/emails/documents), common sense, good manners, old- fashioned etiquette, and demonstrating that you are current in your skills and use of media in a professional way.

A too casual tone or overly familiar writing is a common mistake. Not putting why you would be a good fit for the specific job and company is another area that requires focus in a letter. The cover letter and all writing is a sales pitch of you and your brand, along with why you are the person for this job and company. Besides the writing style and content, the key is know when to write and what to write.

Some mistakes made by candidates include many that involve the cover letter, follow-up emails/letters (or lack thereof) and demonstration that no research was done on the company or the job. Some common mistakes and suggested resolutions include:

Cover letter errors, including; address, spelling, grammar, content and tone in the cover letter that should be written with the resume. The tone should be professional and formal.

The format of the cover letter should be the date, the return name and address, the employer contact name and address, Dear_____ (person's name), and then should follow the format in your own words as follows:

- o *I am applying for X position and I believe I am uniquely qualified for this position (why am I writing and applying?) Identify a few bullet points that indicate how YOU will BENEFIT the company and how YOU will be a fit for the position. (Why me?)*
- o *A brief paragraph on applicable experience; applicable meaning what have you accomplished or what jobs you have done that are similar to or bring experience that is valuable to receiving THIS job offer. (I.e. I have over 5 years of experience working in X industry on Y projects. At Xyz Company, I led a team who achieved 50% response on a marketing campaign. Etc.)*
- o *Indicate specific flexibility (I am willing to schedule an interview at your earliest convenience, I am flexible to travel, I am willing to relocate. If you are NOT flexible, then I recommend you state the items where you are flexible.)*
- o *Run the letter through the spell check and print it and share it with a few people for suggested improvements.*

Common Mistakes Made During Job Application Process:

- Failing to research the company contact name and address so you can personalize the letter.

- Failing to reference your fit for the specific job opening; this includes if they asked for 10 years of experience then you should call out the number of years of experience in the letter, any other requirements that match or are close to a match should be highlighted.

- Poor grammar; what this means is how the sentence flows, using proper English and not repeating the same words over and over and improper use of language in a sentence. If you are not a strong writer, have someone help you. Many people can edit your content so it reads well. Another way to avoid grammatical errors is to keep the sentences short and to the point. No run-on sentences. (Example: I have ten years of experience working in the Healthcare Industry on information systems such as SAS, SAP, HBO and others and I was the lead person on the implementation for the project plans for it. Rather, say, I have ten years of experience working in the Healthcare Industry in the Information Technology areas. I have worked on many different systems including SAS, SAP, HBO and others. I led an implementation effort for the SAS project.)

- No thank you note or follow up process, not persistent in follow-up activities. When you end an interview, you should ask what the next steps are. If they tell you they will contact you, then that isn't a good sign. If they specifically say that the next step is to talk to the VP or another individual, ask when a good time would be to set up this meeting and what the process will be to setup the meeting. This will be either someone will call you or the person you are talking with will arrange it. Get the contact information of both parties; the person you are interviewing with and the person who will call you. You can request they provide a business card or email you a v-card or contact information. You can now send an email follow-up thank you letter. A thank you letter can be sent via email or via the US Mail. As a rule, sending it by 1-2 days after the interview is appropriate. It is a formal letter, not a handwritten note like you might send to a family member. The format is typically:

Dear Mr. or Ms. _____
Thank you for taking the time to discuss the position for _____
You mentioned the key responsibilities and expectations are (3 to 5 things).

I feel that I can meet or exceed these requirements in the following ways (3-5 bullets)
As the follow-up action, you indicated a meeting next week or a phone call.
Please feel free to contact me at phone or email or both at any time. I look forward to
speaking with you soon.
Regards, Your_Name.

- Narcissistic self-centered conversationalist. This is talking too much about yourself and your needs. Even if the interviewer asks you about yourself, your hobbies, your goals, what they really are asking is whether or not you, your personality, lifestyle and personal/career goals align with their company and the position at hand. They really frankly, don't care if you want to have children or like hanging out at the beach and going surfing. Everything you say should emphasize how you view yourself relative to the work environment; will you be eager and flexible or are you a person focused on yourself and your own needs?

- Taking a short term view, rather than a longer term view.
Having some long term goals related to your role in the company and being willing to work to earn a higher title or more responsibility. Ambition is a good thing, but it needs to be couched with humility and willingness to earn the opportunities through performance. This takes time, meaning that 2-4 years in the same job before moving to another within the company is the most common timeframe. Immediate undeserved gratification such as pay raises every year or other expectations that likely won't get met can cause the interviewer to determine you won't be happy. Most companies will give you raises and promotions every 2-4 years. You might have other opportunities to make additional monies based on your performance in the form of profit sharing, stock grants, stock options, bonuses or commissions. The generation of the Baby Boomers who are running these companies have worked their way up and paid their dues with many setbacks. When they see a recent college graduate stating they want to be CEO and make $1 mil per year, they don't see an ambitious person, they see a clueless one. Rather, if you say that short term, you are looking to do _____ (hopefully it's the job you are interviewing for) and you hope longer term to have some opportunities to move around within the company and experience some other roles and responsibilities to really learn the business from all angles. This type of statement shows a willingness to work to get ahead.

- Taking rejection personally: There was someone else who was a better fit. Many positions are filled by internal candidates who have earned their chance. It's likely not that they didn't like you but you may never get any closure on a rejection. You might contact the recruiter or first contact you interviewed with to see if they are willing to provide you constructive feedback to improve your interviewing skills. It never hurts to ask.

- Failure to follow-up and retain the contact: You should ask about future opportunities and ask if you can follow-up every few months to keep in touch. Just contacting the person again every few months shows persistence and a longer term view. They can refer you for new positions or possibly just remain a long term contact for your career. You can then wrap up the next day by providing a concluding email or letter such as thanking them for their time and consideration; stating you are sorry you didn't get the job (Job Title)_____, but hope to stay in touch should other opportunities open up. Say that you will be contacting them in three months to follow up about potential other opportunities that may be a better fit. This way, when you do follow-up (write a reminder in your calendar) they will begin to remember you as someone who follows through on commitments and is persistent.

- If you do get a position elsewhere, you can end the correspondence with a final note letting them know what job you landed and where. I assure you, they will keep your information on file. The new role you landed will give you some experience or skills they might need in the future.

- Failure to let them know you want the job. After the final interview, sending a final note of some kind, reviewing how you left off and what your intentions are. If you are hoping for the offer, state as much in your letter. If you have accepted another role or don't find the job is a fit, you can state the same but indicate that you are still interested in exploring other opportunities at this company in the future.

Rejection, Handling the "No"

It is very difficult for many people to hear the word "no" or be told the job offer went to someone else or they won't be asked back. The best way to handle this "rejection" I've found is to expect it to happen 9 out of 10 times. Meaning, it takes only 1 offer, and in 9 out of 10 interviews, you won't get the job. Look at each interview as a chance to hone your interview skills, request feedback and hopefully get constructive feedback, and make a few new contact(s). You will also learn more about the different jobs and businesses out there, including how they pay and how success is measured and rewarded in these jobs. I believe for most people, this information is very enlightening. Most people have limited experience working at different places, in different industries and in different jobs or roles. This experience will make you wiser and will help your career long term, so look at it as part of a process that includes some rejection.

This brings us down to what skills all employers seem to want in an employee. There are just some types of people who embrace human interaction and face to face meetings, get a lot of information and learn a lot from each meeting, and cement a relationship with someone who might be an asset to their career in the future. Perhaps it's a sense of curiosity and adventure. Each interaction makes you wiser so why not embrace as many interactions, interviews and meetings as possible?

The skills that seem to really excite most employers are:

- Education. A person who speaks and writes in a clear , concise, educated manner. Spelling and Grammar are correct.
- Well read. Can talk about current events knowledgably and industry/company trends with some degree of confidence.
- Strong Sense of Responsibility. This can be reworded as "work-ethic". People who are ethical, honest, responsible, and have integrity are highly valued. These people show up on time, do more than asked, and expect to work hard to earn their way.
- Rainmaker. A rainmaker is a leader. There are many types of leaders. Some are team leads and others are CEOs who run entire businesses. Either way, this is a person others will look to in order to solve a problem. But this is someone who has ideas and can turn them into action. This person usually isn't afraid of failure, they will figure it out. If they have challenges, they view them as obstacles to overcome, not failure.
- Self-Starter and Takes Initiative to Figure things out on their own. The main message communicated by the self-starter is "give me a task or job to do and Ill

figure out how to get it done." They want someone who can function independently without a lot of hand-holding.

- Flexibility. This person doesn't have a fixed idea about working hours, pay plans, or tasks they will and won't perform. They are willing to pitch in to get the job done. This person never states a list of things that they require to be happy. The person focuses on what the business needs to be successful.

- Sense of Urgency. People who work slowly and are meticulous and perfectionists are always valued. However, time is money, and most businesses have deadlines, critical client demands, or other commitments to keep that are time sensitive. People who understand that sometimes you have to switch your schedule to meet demands, or focus on specific tasks quickly will go further than someone who gets it done perfectly but two weeks too late.

- Team Player. This is such an overused term. What companies are really looking for is whether or not you are ok with working on team, with other people, even if at times these people are in conflict. Can you share decision making? Are you a "my way or the highway" kind of person? It's a rare job today when you can work alone and your work stands on its own. Even if you are the star performer, if your business unit is tanking, you will be affected. So the key is to offer up time to mentor, engage with as many people as are necessary to get the job done, and lead the meetings if needed by setting a clear agenda.

- Knows what they want. A person who knows what they want in a job will get what they want. This seems like common sense but many people go for a job search with a list of anything goes. If you know what you want to do for a career, what type of positions where you fit and have experience and value, and clearly understand the pay and demands of such a position, it will be easy for the hiring manager to see the fit. You are also more likely to be happy at a job that you state you want and know why you want it.

Section 4: Got the Job, Now What?

Finally, we are at the last chapter in this book. You have gotten a job and hopefully, you learned from this book and from this process. The things you learned can be used again, and may be needed again in the future. Keep adding to your Linked-in contacts and keep in touch with any good contacts you made. Today's businesses offer little job security for anyone. That means you could get a pink slip (termination) and be told you have to leave that day, because your division is downsizing, being outsourced, or the skills for the position have been changed. You might be notified that you are being put on a performance plan or be given a few months or less to find another job within the company. If you don't find another position within the company, you often have two weeks pay and you are out the door. You won't be given any severance in many places, and no health benefits. It's a bad situation all around.

Not to put a damper on your happiness at the new job, I merely wanted to emphasize that a career is a process, not a job. The process moves you along in your skills, your pay, and eventually opens additional opportunities. Sometimes a pink slip is the opportunity that pushes you to find something you love rather than the job you didn't like or didn't excel. In this section, we cover a few final pointers for a successful career; keeping the job; checking in with yourself on your satisfaction with the job; financial tips; and knowing when the writing is on the wall. These items can help you get through some times when change is coming, is inevitable, and may be uninvited.

Keeping the Job

Finding a job and being hired is only one step. I compare this to having a baby or getting married. This is a major life event, but it is one event in a series of events to determine your career course.
People prepare for a year for a wedding to make it a perfect event. They spend hours on the dress, the shoes, the decorations, the food, the venue, the rehearsal dinner, etc. What they rarely do is spend the same amount of time focusing on working on an equitable and loving cohabitation plan for the marriage itself. Things such as how money will be handled and different philosophies about saving and spending are rarely discussed and negotiated prior to the wedding. How to fairly divide chores is another area. Whether or not to have children and when, and who will stay home with them or care for them?. How many children to have and how to raise and discipline them. Agreement on religious practices. How to spend free time. Views on vacations and where and how to spend them. And so on… So what eventually happens to these couples is a rocky road of discovery, and that in my opinion, is why so many marriages don't last. They think they are committed, but find out that so many differences can't be overcome. This leads to dissatisfaction and frustration in the marriage when one or both parties are unfulfilled.

This same philosophy goes to having a baby. People go to the classes and read the books about what to expect during the birth cycle. They plan the hospital stay and the baby showers. However, they seldom do any research or spend much time figuring out how to care for a baby, how to balance both parents involvement with the baby and overall how to be a good parent. How do you find quality childcare if needed? How do you discipline a two year old versus a 10 year old? I believe if all parents got some training on things to expect and methods to possible handle these situations, there would be less frustration and exhaustion and far less surprises with the parenting process. Unfortunately, few people spend much time on this topic.

Similarly, there is a lot of work in a job search but not much written about job retention and an action plan for keeping the job you acquired. There are some things that can't be controlled, but you don't have to be the "last to know" when the writing is on the wall that your job is being eliminated. If you are ahead of the curve, you can plan and avoid many pitfalls.

Keeping a job today is much harder than finding a job. The reason is that the "real" job is often not the one listed on the job posting. The responsibilities may differ, the people you deal with may be far more difficult than expected, and the pay may even differ as you read in my earlier examples. Sometimes a company is sold to another firm or buys other companies. Suddenly there are three people doing the same job.

Companies also go through hard times and new leaders come into the company. When this happens, they typically bring in their own team. People start "retiring early" or being "reassigned" at the top of the company as the new executives replace them. This team has an approach that may drastically differ from predecessors. There can be extensive micro-management; i.e. looking at every number, every activity, and every expense and asking for ad nauseam documentation and details.

Since none of the above can be predicted or avoided, below are some tips for you to protect yourself and your job longer term:

- **Cast a wide net.** Meet a lot of people and develop some type of rapport with them. Some will be friends, some executives, some mentors, some peers, some acquaintances. If you interact with everyone, i.e. Pick up the phone and call people instead of a text or email, or stop by their desk for a brief hello, eventually you will have a pulse on what is going on in the company. If you hear rumors of an acquisition or change, you might know someone who has a connection and can indirectly ask if they heard of any changes. This is your way of getting ahead of the change, and preparing for it. Additionally, if you are a performer or contributor and it is well known, you are not likely to be eliminated. But if you are new or don't have a great track record, or keep a low profile so that few people know you, it's possible that this network can protect you from elimination or change.

- **Read Read Read.** Read the business magazines and daily business newspaper and keep on top of your industry and other firms that your company partners with. The more you know about what is happening in your industry, how your stock price is doing and why, and what others are saying about your company and industry, the more likely you can predict what your company might do next. If the numbers are bad (i.e. revenue is dropping, the industry has shortages, and work is being outsourced to other countries), it's likely a cost cutting set of measures are forthcoming. What can you do to cut cost or recommend some areas where cost can be cut? Is your job in an area where costs might be cut or jobs outsourced?

- **Expand your skills.** Sometimes you wish you could do something different but are not sure what opportunities exist. The best bet is most firms have a list of job postings that are posted internally first. You can review them and determine if a move makes sense. Every move expands your skills at the company. So it's a good idea to take on new responsibilities even if in the same role. Usually it takes 2-4 years to really master a position. This is a good point in time to ask your boss if you can take on other responsibilities or explore a move within the company. Sometimes, the only thing available is to sit on a committee or two to improve business processes or work on some new project. These are a good way to meet new contacts and expand your understanding of other people's roles in the company, so take advantage.

- **Keep Positive.** A positive upbeat attitude beats a negative downer. It's easy to become depressed and anxious when change is pending. Frustration is common with new systems and processes. Talking bad about it or gossiping will label you as a negative person. People will start avoiding interacting with you as they feel associating with you will bring them down emotionally or worse, will hurt their career. Surround yourself with others whose brand you want to emulate. One of my colleagues, call him Jim, has a moment of complaint, usually one sentence, and then he corrects himself by stating something positive and goes back to the business at hand. I've seen him deflect a complainer by listening for about 30 seconds, then pointedly changing the subject and adding a positive comment at the end to deflect the conversation so it ends on a positive note. An example of this approach went something like this:

Jim told me, "I really don't like how Ted (Jim's Boss) manages because he won't let me drive or handle my own clients, he always steps in and takes over. Its driving me crazy", says Jim, then he said, "I plan to just prove how competent I am so he will back off and anyway, these are good jobs and I plan to be very successful here". This was Jim's way of correcting himself from sounding negative.

An example of how Jim deflected someone else's complaining went something like this, Candy said "I really hate my account list and it's not fair that Ted gives all the good accounts to his favorite boys". Jim Said, "Have you talked to Ted about this, Ted seems like he can be fair and will listen to you". Candy said, "I doubt it would do any good, I mentioned to him I didn't like my accounts and he said he would see what he could do and he did nothing". Jim said, "I plan to make the best of my situation, whether I have good accounts or not. I've found if you just go do the job, people notice and the account list can change. Time is running low, let's get back to reviewing the XYZ account and the call strategy for tomorrow".

If you really need to vent, I always find it helps to have one or two close colleagues who can bounce their concerns off one another. To me this isn't complaining, its expressing feelings about the changes and worries about how your group will be affected. Sometimes these close colleagues are great sources of comfort and ideas. This will also help you get your frustrations out of your system.

The final tip for keeping your job is to make sure you and your immediate supervisor and teammates (defined as those who work closely with you on projects and other activities) provide some regular feedback on how you are doing at the job. This is where the peer review and the manager appraisal process are highly useful. Many companies have these processes, but fail to enforce managers to use them annually or more often. They often can be subjective rather than based on a list of finite measurements. If you don't get these formal documented reviews, then schedule a quarterly meeting with your manager to ask how you are doing and what you need to improve on. This is not a negative discussion but one where you will know in advance how you are viewed and obtain your manager's sponsorship by asking for this review and his/her input.

Checking In With Yourself, Your Goals and Satisfaction With the Job

Too often, time flies and you find yourself in the same job or doing the same thing for many years. You may be flat out sick of the job, or possibly, you like it sometimes and other times you don't. Having career goals, at least 5 years out (longer is great, but many people just don't know what they really want to do long term) is a good thing. Life changes over time, people get married, divorced, have children, are empty nesters, have ill parents or other family members or become ill themselves. All of these events can change your career goals and plans. For example, people who love travel might find they become tired of it after they have children and find they are out of touch with their family. People who thought making a lot of money was important find that they aren't happy with the hours and stress that come with that money making effort. So it's important to "check in with yourself" and see if you still have the same career goals as you did a year before, and if you are on track to achieve them.

One example of this was someone who thought she wanted to move into upper management. She felt most people with her age and experience had high level titles and responsibilities. She kept finding her peers getting younger and younger. Wasn't she promotable? Wasn't she management material? This led to a certain amount of frustration with her lack of upward mobility. Then two things happened, first, she was offered a job managing 20 people. The salary was higher than her salary, but the top end was lower since she would only be paid on the results of this entire team. Her own performance was normally way above the average. So the move didn't pay better, it paid worse in the target income category. Also, the role required she travel constantly and coach people who had 50% of the skill she had. This to her was a highly frustrating thing. She was a "get it done" type of person; she just figured it out. She found that her subordinates either resented her as a manager (didn't want to comply with deadlines and due dates, were disorganized and flat out didn't follow through) or didn't perform and had such a skill deficit that she wasn't sure how to help them and therefore, how she would be successful. I think she finally realized that this move up the chain wasn't necessarily where she would be the most happy or fulfilled.

The second thing that happened was a conversation she had with a friend who had been in management for many years. He pointed out that some people's passion is to be a team leader and other people's passion is to be an individual contributor, which are you? Why are you interested in moving up the chain of command? If you aren't interested, why not? Some traits he indicated he sees in leaders versus contributor types:

Leaders

- Don't like to get into the details of day to day work. Rather like a higher level view or summary level of detail
- Don't like to spend a lot of time putting together reports, in internal meetings with upper management and peer group on schedules, forecasts and budgets.
- Host meetings with subordinates to gather the information needed for these reports and budgets.
- Don't want to get involved in delivering on the steps to complete a task. Rather like to help identify the tasks needed and help keep track of where things are
- Often get involved in problem resolution and escalations within the company, often have to deal with negative situations and deflect them.
- Can be focused up more than down, in "managing the management team" and in managing their expectations. This can involve a combination of political posturing, and self-promotion, or it can involve protecting their subordinates (employees) jobs and shielding them from the internal politics.
- Often would prefer to get more involved in final activity steps, final delivery or launch, final reports, and final deal closings including meeting with clients. They often get "credit" for business successes of their subordinates, so having detail about a specific opportunity or situation makes them appear more involved then they often might be.
- Wants to avoid going into final meetings without clear-cut agenda.
- Takes the risk of not meeting deadlines or making commitments. Is blamed if commitments aren't made and recognized if they are made.
- Has a passion (good managers do) for people and works well with various types of people with different goals and personalities.
- Can enjoy coaching and motivating people.
- Career Goal to move up the chain of command or some managers (not most) are glad to be managers and that is what they want to do. So they might be someone who avoids political posturing.
- A risk-taker who is willing to stick his neck out and take a risk, knowing that some people who do this advance and some lose their job (some managers reach a first line role and have no desire to go higher for this reason.)

Contributors

- Self driven and self-motivated
- Doer, likes to take action and make action happen
- Loves to be recognized and rewarded

- Gets frustrated with incompetent or less skilled people
- Doesn't want or like to deal with internal politics or processes
- Often prefers to be <u>left alone</u> to structure their day and activities or could prefer working on a team or in a small group of other contributors
- Career goals could be to make a lot of money and receive more responsibility only if this is coupled with more money
- May prefer more job flexibility
- Enjoys hands-on work and/or client facing roles.

Of course some people fall in-between or outside of these skills or desires, but ultimately, you end up on a career path of one or the other of these types of jobs. You may feel you are management material and have not had the opportunity to move up the chain of command. In that case, you can only get what you want if you move to a company who either is growing quickly and promoting from within, or is a smaller firm where you can be hired in at the management level. Ironically, some companies just promote people whether that is the career path they want or not. Many contributors make poor managers, often because they lack the people skills or ability to motivate others. Every experienced person has worked for these types of people, and its frustrated and can be a terrible experience. So ultimately, if you can figure out what your manager's style is and what their goals are for their own career, you might build a relationship with this person if they are moving up the chain or at least get them in your court if you want to pursue other options at your company.

I've seen people move up to the top of a larger company, literally running an entire multi-billion dollar organization, only to come crashing down in a reorganization or layoff. Numerous people I know end up at the bottom of another company, literally in entry level roles. These people often became overconfident that they were special and had different skills and that is how they got where they are. The reality, they got where they are due to **sponsorship.** Someone either hired them or sponsored them. The sponsorship is often a great way to get ahead, as long as your sponsor stays at the company or stays in a *position of power.* Should have aspirations to rise to a top position in any company, figure out whose sponsorship you need, who is your boss's sponsor and cast a wide net. Make sure all the potential sponsors and those who could be naysayers know who you are and your aspirations. This takes time, and is often tied to performance (yours or your team's), your manager's sponsor and his/her aspirations to rise up in the business, and who knows you personally and likes you.

There are people put in management jobs running an area of the business they know nothing about, and put policies in place that are bad business and non-motivating. These people don't last too long. They will be typically moved out or aside to a different role over time. So be patient knowing that if someone is a jerk or incompetent at their job, you are not the only one who knows this.

It's important to re-evaluate your goals every few years and measure whether you are closer to meeting them or if they have changed. This is a discovery process, learning about yourself and what you like and don't like over time. Also, what tasks are you really good at doing and what activities do you find are difficult, de-motivating or "not your style"?. Just remembering to set aside some time (hint, put it on your calendar annually) to regroup on
your goals and think about where you are today, what you have achieved and whether or not you are on track to meet your goals will help ensure you don't get "stuck" in your career. These goals also help you to cope when setbacks happen, such as lower pay or being passed over for promotion. In the earlier compensation example, where a major pay cut (couched as a change in compensation plan) took place, it helped to be able to put it into perspective longer term. Short term, it hurt financially, but there were other benefits of the job. The economy was bad and people were out of work. The job had good balance and less travel. I had job security. So comparing it against my goals, I opted to stay and make the best of it.

Financial Tips

Though this is a book about finding and keeping a job, financial tips are probably some of the most important guidance I can provide. It's shocking to me how few people have much financial acumen. Likely their parents didn't have much financial acumen, so they learned from what they saw at home. Money is power and money is freedom. If you have no money or worse, owe money and don't have the ability to pay it back, you lack power and you lack freedom in your life. You are one step away from disaster. So for those who lack financial acumen, I will put a few pointers in here for financial freedom and therefore, career freedom and opportunity. A few facts first:

- Bad credit can hurt your ability to get a job.
- Debt traps people in the jobs they hate or jobs that pay too little.
- Debt prevents people from taking risks to get ahead in life (i.e. getting married, buying a home, start a business, having children, move to a new place, change jobs, make investments that could produce $ money for your future).
- Debt makes people worry and makes them feel hopeless, and then they are more likely to just keep spending because there is no way out anyway.
- Debt and lack of money keep people from reaching their full potential in life.

If you are reading this and already in debt, you missed a few financial lessons in life that I fortunately learned early on.

These financial tips are:

- **Live below your means**. What does this mean? It means you have a NET (not gross) income after taxes and other fees such as healthcare and 401k deposits are removed from your paycheck. Your NET should not include commissions or bonuses that may or may not materialize. It should include only GUARANTEED income. Once you have a net amount, you add up your known expenses, such as loan payments outstanding for cars/student loans/etc, and you end up with what you have to live on, housing/food/transportation cost/utilities/entertainment/and savings if you have no other expected income. What can you afford and still have money left over at end of every month? If housing is a high cost, rent longer rather than buying, or get a roommate and share costs. You will feel richer as a result of this decision. A few other key tips to include in this assessment:

- **Rent versus Buy.** You may be able to buy a low cost home or condominium that fits your budget. You may feel this is a smart move, rather than throwing out money on rent. Ask yourself these questions; Is it really less expensive to buy versus rent? If I use up 20% of my savings for a down payment, pay property taxes, pay utilities, pay for lawn and home repair costs? Is this still a better deal?

a) **Risk.** Even if it is a better deal, there are three major risks to owning a home and they are:

  1. Lack of mobility and flexibility. If your employer offers to move you elsewhere or an opportunity to move comes up, can you afford to move and own this home too?

     Real estate generally is a break even or lost revenue proposition. After you take out a mortgage, your payment is front-end loaded with interest during the first half of your loan period. So if your loan is 30 years, the first 15 years are almost entirely interest payments, and there is little principal or ownership of the home going into that payment. Real estate goes up and down in value. If you add up all the payments through the end of the loan, your often paying 100% more than the value you paid for the home.

     It's hard to sell real estate in a pinch. So that means if you lose your job, most of your expenses will go into paying the mortgage, taxes, repairs, etc, and that puts you at risk of owning an asset that isn't liquid and can drain your savings quickly.

  2. Rentability. If you do have to leave, can you rent it and make a break even or better, a profit on the rental? This would be a definite benefit if the area has a decent amount of rentals and rental income is good. Also, if the house has the ability to allow a rented lower level or basement, this will give you a second income should you end up with no job or personal income.

     With an apartment or rental situation, you can easily leave in a pinch. You may lose your deposit, and you may get into a legal dispute over your lease and be required to make payments, but generally, most apartment complexes will work with you to find someone to help replace you so you can get out of the lease due to hardship.

- **Save a percentage (20% is good) of all the money you make.**
  The 20% would include 6% in your 401k minimally, and higher if you can save more. This will ensure you get the free employee match that many companies offer which is usually about half of the 6% of your total salary. If you don't know how to invest, you can pick a target retirement fund (pick a retirement date) and that will be a mix of stocks and bonds usually a higher stock mix for a younger person than one who has a shorter duration until retirement. Some people say to save more in your 401k, but I personally believe that since this money is only accessible to you by borrowing against the 401k, its best to have other savings to ensure you have ready access to some of your money.

  The remaining money you save can go into a brokerage account with an associated interest bearing savings account. There are some good options available with major brokerage firms that provide a debit/credit card and allow you to receive interest on your savings. This
  money should be invested in a mix of investment types so it can grow with lower risk. Consult a financial advisor regarding the best way to do this (most of the firms who offer these accounts can provide a onetime fee based advice or will provide free online advice.). For example, Charles Schwab has analysis tools that figure out your risk tolerance then recommend a portfolio and selection of stock/bond/asset options. You can then go in and run the tool and track how your investments are doing against various benchmarks and will recommend when to rebalance and redistribute money across investments. Its relatively automated. You can keep some cash and then will have access to your money when or if you need it.

- **Invest what you save in a mix of different types of stocks, bonds, real estate across a balanced portfolio.** The point here is to not just put your money into one stock, it's not a gambling exercise. If you tend to be a bit of a gambler, as a rule, I always assume 10% of my portfolio is for gambling on one or two big hit stocks, the rest is balanced to promote income or appreciation.

- **Pay lower fees for everything.** When you are busy, it's easy to overlook what you are paying in
  fees for all types of things. Among the places where people can overpay and the savings can really add up are:

a) **Credit card fees.** As I mentioned above, debt is bad, and not paying off your card entirely each month can cost you 20% and sometimes more in fees. If you are stuck in credit card debt, move your card balances onto a 0% and no fee card which typically will hold those rates for a year. Pay off the debt or do this again in a year if you are working on a multi-year payoff. Other fees include annual fees. A reward card gives money back but may have a fee annually that exceeds the money you can get back (A percentage of your total spending usually). Look for no fee cards or fees that are far lower than the cash back you could receive.

b) **Groceries.** Clip coupons or subscribe to an online coupon site. This sounds like common sense but people don't bother usually and the savings is literally $5-$25 /week. That really adds up. Shop at discount places when you have to buy basics and take advantage of specials they have that week for BOGO or other discounted items that week where you know you can use them.

c) **Cars and Homes.** Do your homework on big purchases. Use the web to research cars and homes for sales and comparable pricing. Show up armed with information about what features you expect and what price you should pay based on this research. Take your time, don't buy on a whim. For example, we recently shopped for a car and visited many dealers to determine which car we wanted. They all wanted to close the sale, but we really hadn't finalized which car type we wanted. After we escaped from the sales people in some of these dealerships, we went home and researched the car we wanted, the color we wanted and the features we wanted through Internet sites. We gathered information on what the car cost the dealer and suggested retail price, along with realistic trade in values for our old car.

We then submitted through the web to be contacted by dealers who had this car in stock and got pricing sent to us via email along with trades for our old car that were estimated value (pending seeing the trade-in car). We found dealers in other states who were willing to provide the cars for a lower cost. We went back to the local dealer with this information and they matched the cost and obtained the car through their own network. Savings of at least $5000-7000 on the car, free features provided on the car they did have in stock or available for us (things like racing stripes or upgraded rims) and an additional $2000 for our trade in than we were offered at the dealer prior.

For homes, it's a little more difficult to obtain a bargain. A good realtor can provide information on what the current pricing is in a neighborhood or whether or not a home has been on the market a while or is a new listing. The best bet for home shopping is to know what you can and want to afford and don't go over the amount you can afford. Make sure you are preapproved for a loan and have the 20% down payment. This makes the seller more motivated to sell to you, as you are less likely to cancel the sale. They might be more likely to accept a lower offer from you knowing you qualify. Contrary to advice you will get from the real estate agent, making an offer that is too low ISNT a bad idea. You don't know the situation with the seller, whether they are desperate or not or out of time and just want to end the sales effort. There is a strategy here that we use in sales, it's called "qualification" meaning, find out the bottom line of what someone is willing to spend before trying to put a deal together for a client. In this case, the deal will benefit the buyer, not the seller, so you need to figure out their bottom line. There are two approaches you can take that I have used that work for getting the best deal.

- *Test the Water:* ask your agent that if you made an offer for _____ with no contingencies preferably (i.e. you don't have to sell another home first or obtain a loan approval) but you can have an inspection contingency but agree to waive minor repair fees, would the buyer consider that offer. She/he might tell you to write it up, but don't do it. Find out if they are willing to sell for 10% less or 20% less (usually not lower than 20% less). Tell your agent that you are considering an offer but don't feel the home is worth the amount being asked for the following reasons. She/he might resist but insist that before you make an offer you want to know if it's not going to be considered. Your agent will call the selling agent and ask and in turn, the selling agent will find out if the offer is ok or not. They may come back and say, "make the offer and we will consider it" or "we won't tell you until you make an offer". But more likely, the agents will talk and determine if the price is ok with the seller or not and let you know. At that point, you can make the offer or make the offer a few thousand under the original amount. This might make the seller angry, but at that point, you know they are willing to come down and you are haggling over only a few thousand dollars. You can end up at your original offer this way and appear to be making a concession.

- *Offer Alternatives.* People are more likely to consider offers if they are presented as options, i.e. more than one option. Using the same approach as above, you might come up with two or three different offer options. For example, we might offer X if the seller throws in the furniture, and Y if they don't throw in the furniture. Or you might indicate a cosmetic (carpet) or major repair or appliance warranty is included in one option, and the lower offer has no contingency other than major repairs at the inspection. Don't waive the inspection because major repairs include termite damage, structural or sink hole, and broken items (i.e. water heater doesn't work) and that can cost you thousands. A few pieces of siding to be replaced or a small repair that requires a few hundred dollars can be waived.

- **Drive a car until the car costs more to repair then its worth.** There are times when a new car is a better deal than a used car. This is when you have a long warranty and there are a lot of incentives to buy new, and when used cars are almost as much in cost as new cars. Typically, we buy a car that is one year old and under 20,000 miles or we buy a new car when the dollars are roughly the same, but we drive our cars for 10-12 years or until they hit 75,000 to 100,000 miles. This allows us to have no car payment for the bulk of the years we own it. We do the regular maintenance and don't buy the extended warranties. Additionally, auto parts have a huge (300% sometimes) mark up and labor is very high and overpriced if you haven't noticed. One way to resolve this is for things where you know what the part will be (such as a new fender), you can order online from a wholesaler and have it installed at your local mechanic or Tire Kingdom store. I once was told it was $600 to repair a scratched and dented front fender on a Toyota. I found the part of $180 on line and the Tire Kingdom installed it for $70, total cost $250.

- **Pay cash rather than credit.** If not, pay off all your credit card bills every month in full. Only buy what you can afford to pay back in one month.

- **Carry only one or two credit cards.** Refuse the store card offers, even if your savings today is 10-15%. Use cash back cards when possible that have no annual fee. Store credit cards may seem like a great deal when they save you 15% off this purchase but nothing off any future purchases. I've had the cashier advise me to open the account then when the card comes, cut it up and don't use it again. This is a bad idea. You end up with a line of credit on that card and it shows up in your credit report. If anyone should steal your identity, they could use that card and you wouldn't find out until the bill came. My recommendation is not to bother. Rather, use coupons when you shop if they are available. Before you go to a store, look in the paper and online for coupons and print them out. If you do shop exclusively somewhere that has a card that offers discounts for card members only, it may be worth having a card for just that store. As a general rule, I don't carry these exception cards around in my wallet. I keep them in a safe place and use them only when I go shopping at the store. This protects you in case of your wallet being lost or stolen.

- **Put 20% down minimally when buying a home.** If possible, take out a 15 year loan or pay more monthly or yearly on a 30 year loan to retire the principal. Do NOT ever borrow against your home. If you don't have the 20%, then wait until you do to buy a home. Under 20% requires a higher credit score, will charge a higher set of fees, and may require Private Mortgage Insurance (can add 10% or more to the payment). The only exception would be if there is a special first time homebuyer exclusion or other benefit offered by a government lender. You may think, Ill refinance later, but the truth is, you probably will have to pay additional fees to refinance and will end up starting all over again on interest payment. People don't realize that this mortgage payment can be a major rip-off. You literally spend the first half of any mortgage term playing mostly interest. If you are 5 years into a 15 year mortgage, you will start all over again, paying mostly interest the first half of the new mortgage. It's better to ask your lender if they have a modification program, where for a fee, they just lower your interest payment for the remaining term of your mortgage OR optionally, pay down your principal with extra money every month or annually (i.e. a bonus payment or tax refund could go to reduce your principal which is amount owed on the home itself without fees or interest.). This way your payment starts to go down and your principal goes up.

- **Don't give the Government your money.** I don't mean to not pay your taxes owed. Of course you pay required taxes. But what I mean by this is a tax refund means you overpaid your taxes and you get the money back four months after the year ends that you overpaid. If you could have invested or saved that money every month rather than paid the government, you could have made the 4% minimal return or more. Instead you just got back what you paid. You are required to pay at least what you paid the year before or you can get a penalty payment added to your tax bill. So take a look at a few years of returns and ask your accountant what number of deductions you should take to pay the minimal taxes required with a target to not owe and not get a refund. You may be off somewhat, but either way, it's better than giving the government a free loan of your money. Some tax savings tips:

- Pay attention to how taxes are paid and for what types of things. If you have a sales tax holiday in your state, use it to buy things you need.
- If you pay only 15% on capital gains for investments owned over a year, don't sell stocks until a year has gone by otherwise you pay your full income tax amount on that gain. You can net short term losses against short term gains, and long term losses against long term gains. You can carry forward up to $3000 of losses if you lost more than you gained each year.
- If you are in a high tax bracket, consider tax free municipal bonds or dividend paying stocks (if Dividend taxes are still low).
- If your property taxes are out of line with your current home value, call the property appraisers office or have an independent appraisal done ($200-500) and use that to get a lower property tax rate. Be conscious of how much you are paying to the government, whether in state and local taxes or in federal taxes.
- Some money to charity or donate items and keep an itemized receipt. Do this every year. You can take a deduction for some of the value of the items, depending on your tax bracket.
- If you have a light head for these details, ask a tax adviser to give you a list of areas where you might save on your taxes.

- **Know how much money you have and how much you owe off the top of your head**. If you don't know this, then make sure all your money is in the same place so it's easy to figure out. You might have a 401k and an online broker/banking account combo. An On line brokerage with associated bank account is a great option. You can login from anywhere and figure out exactly how much money you have for both the 401k and the brokerage/bank account combo. Balance your checkbook, make sure you know where and how you are spending your money. Even if you aren't going to do an exact balance, write down your withdrawals and the checks you write and the amount and you can round these for an approximate total. You can true up at month end using the online records. This is better than not having a clue how much money you have in your account.

- **Talk with your spouse or partner and make sure they agree with you on the plan above.** If not, create a plan that you can both live with that helps you reach your financial goals. *Set financial goals.* How much realistically will I need to retire? When can or when would I like to retire? How much do I have to save in order to meet these goals? Make sure your plan allows for some emergencies like sudden expenses for medical, or savings to cover costs (6 months to a year or longer) should you lose your job. Do not base your plan on unreasonable returns on investment or savings goals that cant likely be met. Rather make them very conservative (return of 4% annually on average) or savings of 10-20% of your money to start. That way, you will be pleasantly surprised at the end if you get a better return.

If you fall on bad times hopefully you had a plan and weren't completely wiped out. But if you did fall on hard times, such as lost a job and have only three months to find a new one or you can't pay your bills, do something about that day 1. Put your home for sale, rent it out, and move in with a friend of parents to conserve cash. Don't wait until you run out of time or options. Assume the worst (it may take years to find a new job) and when it turns out ok, you can regroup and get back on track. One thing that really helps is if you and your spouse have vastly different financial management skills, i.e. one is a spender and the other a saver, its best to create a budget and allow the spender some flexibility to spend out of special account for that purpose. You can figure out together what you can afford for clothing, luxury items, haircuts, golf, etc, and put that into a separate account so that it can be used for these items.

Savings should be set up to be automated so it's taken out of your savings account or paycheck automatically, that way, you won't fall victim to spending more than planned.

The Writing is On the Wall

I want to end this book on a positive note. Seeing the writing on the wall and knowing when to take action because your job is at risk IS a positive note. You probably thought that was a negative thing, after all, it means, likely you are going to lose your job.

Seeing the situation before it happens to you and planning for it will allow you can get ahead of the curve and create a better opportunity for yourself before it's too late. Don't get too comfortable or complacent. Earlier I indicated that once you get a job, In order to keep the job, you need to stay on top of the industry, the company financials and growth plans, and your own role in the company. You need to network within the company so that if there are cutbacks, someone will either rescue you or possibly offer you another place in the company. You need to seek out opportunities for new roles or responsibilities so you have more contacts and all around more skillsets to tap into in the case of a layoff or reorganization. If you can see that the group you are in is falling apart, but it's not the last month before the place implodes, you can seek out a different job at the company. You can go to the internal job search site and look to see what jobs are posted as open. Better, if you know a lot of people, you can reach out to one or two of your contacts and say you really want to work in their team or group, will there be any openings coming up? They will tell you if they have planned for openings or when they will know for sure. You will be first in line and first to interview and potentially, already in mind for the role so the request could be written so you are the obvious candidate (i.e. Prefer a specific location and you happen to live there, or other types of skills you bring to the table that are unique). People will wonder how you are like a cat, always landing on your feet. This is how you do it!

If there is nothing else for you to do at your current firm, start the job search using this book as a guideline. You probably know a lot more people now. You have used Linked-in with your clients, colleagues and employed friends and a lot of new recruiters who reached out to you for jobs you didn't want, but you still kept in touch. If people leave your company to move on to other jobs, immediately link to them and keep that connection. Hopefully, you joined a few professional organizations and got a few contacts there. You can tell all your contacts (one on one, no broadcast) you are still at XYZ but looking for a new challenge and are interested in exploring options. People hire people who are employed more often than the unemployed. It's not fair but it's a fact of life.

Good Luck to You

I hope this book was helpful to you and maybe it was the reason you found a job and are financially more secure. I hope so. I wrote the book because I have two college students, plus many others have reached out to me looking for help with resumes, contact names at companies where I have worked and others, along with requested a personal reference. When I ask what they are looking to do or what they have done to find a job, I found a shocking lack of knowledge on what they should do beyond lob applications to a web site or advertisement. People got depressed after a few weeks, and just gave up on the job search. I also found what I define as a deplorable lack of etiquette, such as informal writing or lack of follow-up or thank you letters. It seems that their parents haven't advised them on their resume, the job search process, etiquette or financial matters. It appears many parents or schools don't know how to do this, as many have worked for years in the same place or same field and never had to worry about finding new jobs.

Lucky for me (I now see it), I worked in Technology where there is constant change, constant new skills, little job security, and opportunity to get ahead if you make the right career choices at the right time. So I learned how to find a job and did it about 10 times over a long career spanning 30+ years. Changing proactively, I learned to take and keep control of my own career. I started with local recruiters in my industry and newspaper ads and worked my way into Social Media and other sources. I learned a lot along the way, and I attempted to share that knowledge in this book. I also asked several other people to read this and provide their input, people who also have had to find jobs during a down economy and were successful. What I found is that they often deployed many of the recommendations listed in this book, believed in themselves and kept a positive attitude, and finally they didn't give up easily. Some of the stories in this book come from them, and their experience.

Not being able to find any job is a terribly depressing thing for someone who is first starting out. This is especially terrifying to someone just graduating or a few years out of college. This book is intended to create a process for new job seekers to follow that will lead to job hunting success.

Someone who has had a job knows at least they did a good job for many years and knows they have skills that have been useful at one time. This book might help them to regroup on new tools for finding a job today and refresh their memory on the process.

About the Author:

Nancy Schreimann lives in Florida, is married and has two college student children. She has worked in professional sales, management, and business partner development roles for over 28 years for a variety of companies, large and small, public and private.

A special thanks to all who contributed to this book, including Joyce Katz, my mother who is a veteran retired teacher and she provided editing assistance with this book. A loving call out to the real inspiration for this book, Race and Shayne Schreimann, my son and daughter who are currently attending college and hope to graduate and find a career that is inspiring and fruitful. If not for them, I would not have been motivated to write this knowledge down for the benefit of anyone, but especially, new graduates and those who are looking for jobs and often struggle to find one. Possibly, they may now avoid so many pitfalls and mistakes, and have long and successful careers.

www.ingramcontent.com/pod-product-compliance
Lightning Source LLC
Chambersburg PA
CBHW060618210326

41520CB00010B/1383